My Uncle Al would have loved this book.

Deirdre Capone

✳

If you're a Vegas nut, like we are, you won't put it down.
Bruce Martin, Producer, On the Felt radio
www.MLPoker.com

✳

Hearing Las Vegas tales from the '50s and '60s is far more fascinating than hearing stories about other cities during the same years. This is mostly because the players all have nicknames like "Bugsy," "Icepick," and "The Ant," and their real-life activities were more outrageous than the endless fiction they continue to inspire. If *The Sopranos* is entertaining, true stories from the years when the Mob ran Vegas are downright enthralling. . . .

When the Mob Ran Vegas is a unique glimpse into the past that shaped Las Vegas into what it is today. Whether you find it nostalgic or shocking, whether you wish those days could return or are happy they've vanished into the past, Fischer has created a picture of an era that preserves not only faces and facts, but also a personal impression of a city he clearly loves.

Megan Edwards, Living Las Vegas

✳

The world needs guys like you keeping a record. Publishing your research helps many future generations.

David G. Schwartz, Coordinator, Gaming Studies Research Center, University of Nevada, Las Vegas

✳

WHEN THE MOB RAN VEGAS

STORIES OF MONEY, MAYHEM AND MURDER

STEVE FISCHER

Berkline Press
www.WhenTheMobRanVegas.com
Omaha, Nebraska

To my parents,
Bernie and Dorothy Fischer,
who passed their love of Vegas on to me

On the front cover: Virginia Hill, upper left corner; mug shots, left to right, Little Moey Sedway, Steve Fischer, Marshall Caifano, Tony Accardo, Frank "Lefty" Rosenthal, Meyer Lansky, Tony Spilotro; death scene, Bugsy Siegel.

On the back cover: Lisa Malouf Medford in a 1961 photo at the Tropicana, the first nude showgirl in Las Vegas. Photo by the legendary Michael Nagro.

© 2005, 2006, 2007, Steve Fischer
ISBN 10: 0-9770658-0-4
ISBN 13: 978-09770658-0-6

Fischer, Steve 1943-
   When the mob ran Vegas: stories of money, mayhem
and murder / Steve Fischer
   p. cm.
   Includes bibliographical references and index.

   1. Las Vegas (Nev.)—History—20th century—
Anecdotes. 2. Las Vegas (Nev.)—Social—Social life and customs
—20th century—Anecdotes. 3. Organized crime—Nevada—
Las Vegas—History —20th century—Anecdotes.
4. Nineteen fifties. 5. Nineteen sixties. I. Title.
F849.L35F575 2005   979.3'13504
          QB105-600177

20 19 18 17 16 15 14 13

Published by Berkline Press. For more information about this book, to order the book, and to contact the author, go to www.WhenTheMobRanVegas.com.

Cover design by LA Design Co.

Desktop production by Freestyle Graphics

Editorial services of Write On, Inc.

Marketing and publicity by Concierge Marketing

CONTENTS

ACKNOWLEDGMENTS

This could very well be the first book ever created from eBay listings. I'd like to thank the hundreds of eBayers who've made the writing of this book as much fun as it has been. Thanks for your kind and supportive emails.

Many others helped me put this book together:

Thanks to **Deanna DeMatteo** for immense research assistance over the past few years. Recognized as the most complete and well-researched compendium of information available is Deanna's Web site lvstriphistory.com. A special thank you for the countless hours of research on the Tony Cornero biography.

"History turns to dust, and I'm here to collect that dust and turn it into something called a story ... which is what I do when I take people on a tour of my collection." A quote from **Howard Klein,** one of the true experts on the evolution of the Las Vegas Strip, Howard has put together a world-class collection of Las Vegas history. With thanks for your friendship, your knowledge, and all you've done for this book.

John Neeland, Publicity Manager of the Riviera Hotel in Las Vegas, has been a pleasure to work with on this project. John and his staff at the Riviera have supplied me with many of the photos for the book. After nearly 40 years in the business, there are not a lot of headliners with whom he hasn't worked, or stories he doesn't know.

I don't know if there's an author who writes about Las Vegas who doesn't speak with **Howard Schwartz** of the Gamblers Book Shop and the famous GBC (Gamblers Book Club) in Las Vegas. His knowledge of the personalities of Las Vegas is legendary.

Bob Stoldal is News Director of KLAS TV, General Manager of Las Vegas One TV, and a man who enjoys the history of Las Vegas as much as I do. Bob's specialty is the Las Vegas of the early Twentieth Century, from 1900 through 1931, and he's the recognized expert in that field. Bob is Chairman of the Nevada State Museum Board, and Chairman of the City of Las Vegas Historical Preservation Commission.

Steve Cutler, collector, historian and founder of the Casino Legends Hall of Fame, gets a special "thank you." Steve and his wife, Sheryl Slakoff, seem to know everyone in Las Vegas. And they were kind enough to open doors for me that I would never have been able to enter were it not for them.

Thanks to Stephen D. Fitt, Ph.D., Instructional Librarian UNLV, for all his assistance on this project. Thanks to casino legend Bernie Sindler.

And also, thanks to Richard Greeno, a leading authority on Benny Binion and the El Rancho Vegas. To Dick Taylor, author and historian. Dick was GM of Hacienda for many years, and the Last Frontier in the late '50s. To *Casino Chip and Token News Magazine*, especially to Allan Anderson, editor, and to Jim Steffner, Dick Covington, and Mike Quinlivan. And to Paul Reed, for sharing his knowledge of what *really* happened when the Mob ran Vegas.

Thanks to Jeff and Corky Bleaman, Esther Meiches, John Zipay, Jay Kiran, Veronica Worth, Skip Harouff, Paul Wagner, Jim Brown, Ross Conquest, Vikki Celaya and my friend, the now ex-Mobster in Las Vegas.

To my two kids and four grandkids, I told you that eventually I'd be finished with the book, and then Mom and I could start babysitting again. I'll let you know when the book is finished.

And to my wonderful wife, Jan, thanks for the hundreds of hours of work you put in on this book, and the 40 years that you've put up with me.

Of course I've forgotten people who should have been thanked for their assistance, and I apologize. Your names will be mentioned in Book 2 because chances are I'll be asking for some more assistance.

INTRODUCTION

What is it about Las Vegas that captivates us historians? Is it how the skim worked at the Stardust and how millions of dollars walked out of the door uncounted? Or what really happened when Frank Sinatra threw a chair at the casino boss of the Sands? Did you ever hear the story about how some very bad Vegas guys rigged the gin rummy games at the Friars Club and took a bunch of famous people to the cleaners? Howard Hughes had some weird notions about the Silver Slipper and put his money where his paranoia was. It's all Vegas, and it is fascinating history.

Las Vegas in the '50s and '60s was indeed another world. Those were the days when small-time gamblers like me, in town with my wife for a weekend of shows and great food, could ride down the elevator at one of the Strip hotels with Lucille Ball, have an A table at the Versailles Room at the Riviera to see Rowan and Martin, with Edie Adams opening, and laugh until it hurt when Buddy Hackett played the old Congo Room at the Sahara.

Behind the scenes, the Mob ran Vegas in those days. And stories abound. Through years of study and interviews and just talking to people from all strata of Las Vegas comes this book, a glimpse into the money, mayhem, and murders of the Las Vegas of just a few years ago.

Even though I have put together an impressive collection of memorabilia from Las Vegas, I tell people that I'm a collector of Las Vegas stories.

Back in May 2003, I discovered a new audience for my stories on the wonderful world of eBay. Newly retired, I knew I should start getting rid of some of the stuff I'd collected over the years. But what I wanted to do was sit down and write. I had three things going for me: I had plenty of time on my hands, a very large collection of Las Vegas memorabilia, and a million Las Vegas stories that I'd share at the drop of a hat.

My first time selling on eBay, I stayed up through the night composing my first eBay listing. Never mind the item, it was the story behind it that captivated eBay browsers. Here was a chance to share some of the great stories I know about Las Vegas and make a few bucks in the process.

Item one was a 1952 Tariff Sheet from the newly opened Sands Hotel. A "Tariff Sheet" was a list of room prices at the Sands, and a Gala New Year's Eve Party at the Sands, welcoming in the year 1953.

I enjoy research, and I knew who the licensed owners of the Sands were, and who the hidden owners of the Sands were. In presenting the 1952 Tariff Sheet in the context of who owned the Sands when it first opened, and who was behind the people who owned the Sands when it first opened, I ended up writing a story, which I totally enjoyed sharing with anyone who would see the item on eBay.

To my great surprise, I got two emails the following morning. Both of them were extremely complimentary. Neither of the writers bid on the Tariff Sheet, but they both said they enjoyed reading about the hidden owners of the Sands, like Doc Stacher, a Mob boss from New Jersey. I wrote both of them, thanked them for their nice emails, and began writing this book.

The Sands Tariff Sheet itself was won by a fellow who's been a regular client of mine since I started on eBay. You'll notice a couple of the illustrations in this book are credited to the Conquest Collection. That's my very first customer's collection. And the winning bid for the Tariff Sheet was $63.00.

Over the past few years and hundreds of eBay listings during that time, I've met many people who love Las Vegas history as much as I do. As an added bonus, I've met a large number of other collectors and historians who've become friends.

Many of the stories you'll read are about famous or infamous people, many are about people you've never heard of before, but they all contributed to giving this fabulous town such a vibrant history.

Steve Fischer

THAT DAMN KEFAUVER COMMITTEE

From March 13 to March 30, 1951, the living room at our house was the place to be. Uncle Jack and Aunt Thelma were over, and our next-door neighbors, Mr. and Mrs. Annunziata showed up every day around 5. They'd all sit on folding chairs and the couch.

My dad and uncle insisted that we kids watch it also. "It's history in the making," dad used to say before the show began each day. The New York City schools let the seniors go home early to watch the hearings. It's "Democracy in Action."

The day before the televised committee meetings began in the Federal Courthouse in lower Manhattan, on March 12, United States Senator Estes Kefauver from the great state of Tennessee was on the front cover of *TIME* magazine. He was a national celebrity. He was making his final stop in his crusade to free America from the horrors of "Organized Crimes in Interstate Commerce."

First, a little explanation about the Senate committee:

The Senate Committee on Organized Crime in Interstate Commerce needed a chairman. Nobody particularly wanted the committee assignment; 1951 was a year away from a Presidential and the Senatorial elections – and you could just get buried chairing some stupid committee on the Organized Crime in Interstate Commerce. That was just not a wise election year issue.

There was another committee out there looking for a Chairman that interested Estes – a much sexier committee – something that would get him into the limelight. Being the junior Senator from Tennessee was OK, but Estes Kefauver had his sights set on higher office. The problem was that damn, drunken, loudmouth from Wisconsin, also a junior Senator, who didn't have one day's more seniority than Estes, was already campaigning to get on the House Un-American Activities Committee (HUAC). But when Joe McCarthy got that plum of a job, Senator Kefauver took over as chairman of the Organized Crimes in Interstate Commerce Committee. After a little study, he thought maybe he could do something with this committee after all.

The original charge of the committee as defined by chairman Senator Kefauver was to "combat any type of organized crime which spilled over state boundaries. Such crimes include drug trafficking, the smuggling of cigarettes or liquor on which no taxes had been paid, theft, hijacking, extortion, kidnapping, pornography, stock manipulation and stock fraud, prostitution and bond fraud."

There were also some unspecified crimes, all having to do with stopping commerce that was crossing "interstate boundaries for illegal purposes."

That is all pretty laudable stuff, right?

What they ended up investigating had next to nothing to do with interstate commerce, it had to do with illegal gambling. Not wire gambling – not bookmaking, which does go interstate. We're talking about slot machine operators, casinos with tuxedoed croupiers spinning roulette wheels, and poker games. I don't mean to minimize the work that the committee did, and it provided a lot of entertainment for a lot of people who had never seen a real Mobster before. It also brought to light "revelations" as it described them – about gambling in America – of course, these revelations were about illegal gambling clubs that had been operating completely out in the open for the past 20 years or so.

Although Kefauver's committee visited a total of 14 different cities – Kefauver's home state of Tennessee certainly had its share of gambling parlors and vice, and all the same kinds of activities that went on in most of the other stops in Kefauver's Crusade – yet Tennessee was never looked at by the committee. All the Memphis bookmakers were safe as long as 'ol Estes was in charge of the committee, apparently.

And it was great drama, whether it was posturing or not. Television was in its infancy, and the Kefauver committee caught the nation's interest. Not only was our living room crowded – we had one of those 9-inch Philco televisions – my dad bought a large magnifying glass that you installed over the screen so it was like watching TV on a 9 -1/2-inch screen.

Joey Adonis, "I likes ya, youse can call me Joey A," testifies before the Kefauver Committee. He refused to testify against himself "in any respect."

Frank Costello, whom the committee had called "The Prime Minister of Organized Crime in America," was questioned every single day the committee was in New York – sometimes for 10 minutes, sometimes for an hour, but every single day.

And every day, Frank Costello sat there, saying, "On advice of counsel, I decline to answer on the grounds that it may incriminate me."

Finally his lawyer complained to the committee that it wasn't fair to his client to keep focusing on his face during this interrogation. So the pool cameraman for WPIX New York focused on Costello's hands – and so did my parents along with 30 million other people – as this Mafia *capo* was being grilled by the Senators. And the camera remained focused on his hands during the questioning about the Mafia. Very dramatic stuff.

Q: "Are you, Mr. Costello, in charge of the United States Mafia?"

A: "On advice of counsel, I decline to answer on the grounds that it may incriminate me."

Q: "Mr. Costello, do you know Joe Bonnano or Guisseppe Profaci or Carlos Marcello or Meyer Lansky?"

A: "On advice of counsel, I decline to answer on the grounds that it may incriminate me."

Q: "Mr. Costello, did you have breakfast this morning at the Algonquin Hotel coffee shop with known Mafia Chieftain Louis Santos, also known as Santo Trafficante?"

A: "On advice of counsel, I decline to answer on the grounds that it may incriminate me."

Costello's raspy, gravely voice, (the result of an accident when a surgeon mistakenly singed his vocal cords as a child), was heard on every TV in America. It became the model for the Marlon Brando voice in the *Godfather*.

Q: "Mr. Costello, you were seen having breakfast with Mr. Traficante this morning. Apparently you had ordered oatmeal and toast. Was the oatmeal any good?"

(Here Frank Costello leaned back and behind his hand conferred with his $300-an-hour attorney, George Wolf. The whispered conversation lasted about 30 seconds.)

A: "On advice of counsel, I decline to answer on the grounds that it may incriminate me."

In five days, Frank Costello took the Fifth a total of 138 times.

On the sixth day that he was called into the Federal Courthouse in New York to be grilled by Senator, and soon-to-be-running-for-Vice President Estes Kefauver, Costello decided that with or without advice of counsel, he'd had it up to here!

When the committee came back from lunch at 1:00 p.m., (they had made Costello report at 9:00 a.m), they got around to calling him up to the table to testify.

Q: "Good afternoon, Mr. Costello, how are you today?"

A: "You know something, Senator? This whole circus of yours is just wasting my time. Go stick it in your hat!"

With that, Frank Costello, who in 1951 was *capo di tuti capi* in the US, walked out on Senator Estes Kefauver and his whole damn committee, right on live TV!

Frank Costello storming off. The Kefauver Committee required him to be there every single day the committee was in session, and to report each morning at 9 a.m. Many days Costello wasn't called on until 3 p.m. though he'd been there since 9 a.m.

From that moment on, *Mafia* became a word known in every household in America.

Two short notes here:

- "Go stick it in your hat" is a paraphrase of what Mr. Costello really said, and

- Even though Frank Costello felt good for the rest of the day, walking out on that stupid committee, on Aug. 15, 1952, he was sentenced to 18 months in prison for contempt of the US Senate. He was released Oct. 29, 1953.

What Kefauver and his committee did was to stir the American public's awareness and fascination with the Mafia.

Besides Frank Costello being subpoenaed, Meyer Lansky was served with a subpoena (the third time he was told to appear before the committee), as was Joey Adonis ("Joey A" to his friends), and so was Virginia Hill...

This anecdote is absolutely true. I'm sure there's a moral in here somewhere, but I'm not sure what it is.

To set the scene –

First, this is live TV, you know, the kind that you don't get a chance to edit.

Virginia Hill, who was Bugsy Siegel's main squeeze, was now married and living in Austria. She'd come to New York to shop, was seen, and was served with a subpoena to appear before the Kefauver committee.

This is only four years after Bugsy was shot, and the American public knew who Virginia Hill was, but had only seen her picture in the papers. The television public was now going to get a chance to watch her sweat under the questioning of Senator Estes Kefauver, protector of The Flag, Mom's Apple Pie, and Virtue of Living in an America Free of Mobsters – all on live TV!

Virginia Hill during screen test. Age 24,
height 5'4", weight 116 lbs.

WPIX, a local independent station in New York, was picked to do the feed. They had three cameras covering the committee, and the three networks NBC, CBS, and ABC picked up their images from WPIX and spread them nationwide. When the Kefauver committee took a break for lunch, the rest of the country took a break for lunch – this was fabulous free entertainment.

"I can't wait to see that floozie on TV, I heard she has lovers all over the world...and you know she made Bugsy leave his wife and two daughters for her, the slut!"

And when Virginia Hill was about to face the committee at 6:30 p.m., we all sat down in front of the Philco to watch her while eating dinner. History in the making, you know!

Never one to be shy about anything, and also known for her, well, call it extremely salty language, she easily handled questions about the death of Bugsy Siegel.

She played around with the committee for a while, and insisted that neither she, nor her brother Chickie Hill, who was in the house, nor her maid, who was in the house, nor Allen Smiley, who was in the house – "knows nuthin' about nuthin' about Ben's death, Senator."

Then Senator Estes Kefauver made a mistake. He began asking Virginia Hill about her income.

How come she was given so much money by so many men, he wanted to know.

There was the doctor in Chicago, and the two Mobsters in New York, and Ben Siegel, and the millionaire in Mexico, and the New York concert violinist – all giving her money over the years, for no apparent reason.

"How come that's the case, Miss Hill?" Kefauver asked. She demurred once. Kefauver pushed, and she replied,

HILL: "Senator, are you SURE you want to know why these men give me money?"

KEFAUVER: "Of course I want to know, Miss Hill."

HILL: "Senator, they give me money, because I'm the best damn cocksucker in the United States!"

[The unexpected answer according to observers, knocked the toupee off Senator Charles W. Tobey, and had parents all over the country choking on meat loaf and string beans.]

The next day, the boys in Miss Hildreth's 8th grade class decided that the Kefauver committee hearings was their favorite TV show of all time.

The 14 cities that the committee traveled to, and held hearings in, were Washington, D.C., Tampa, Miami, New York City, Cleveland, St. Louis, Kansas City, New Orleans, Chicago,

Detroit, Philadelphia, Los Angeles, San Francisco, and, of course, Las Vegas.

The committee covered 52,000 miles and heard from more than 600 witnesses.

In Las Vegas, nearly every one of the 1950 Las Vegas casino owners and operators was called to testify.

By the time the committee ended in April 1951, 86 percent of American homes were watching the hearings religiously. Overnight, millions of Americans knew the name Kefauver along with Jake "Greasy Thumb" Guzak, Charlie "Trigger Finger" Fischetti, Tony "Big Tuna" Accardo and others.

However, besides providing free, jaw-dropping entertainment to the American public for months, the Kefauver hearings were also responsible for one more thing.

Because of the Kefauver committee's visibility, local city councils and sheriffs were pressured to get the non-licensed casinos closed up across America. And some of the best and brightest gaming people in the world loaded their kids and wives in their Cadillacs, said goodbye to the winters in Minneapolis and began amassing fortunes, nearly completely legally.

BUGSY SIEGEL'S FLAMINGO
September 13, 1945

Folsom's Guest Cottages on US Highway 91, six miles south of Las Vegas, closed in 1941.

Harold Folsom had died and his widow, Maggie, just couldn't run the place. It used to be a nice place. Right on the Los Angeles Highway, only about 4 miles south of town, other side of the highway from that new El Rancho Las Vegas place they were building. Another mile or so south of there, right where the highway takes a bend.

One day, Maggie received a long distance call from a Mr. Bautzer who said he was an attorney in Los Angeles. Mr. Bautzer asked Maggie if she'd ever thought of selling the Guest Cottages.

There were some back taxes due, but if Maggie were interested, a real nice deal could be worked out. Mr. Bautzer said he had a client who wanted to buy the old, run-down place. And the client would pay off the delinquent taxes, and, well, "What would you say to $8,000 additional for you?" Maggie was afraid that Mr. Bautzer could hear the war whoop she let out.

After Mr. Bautzer hung up, Maggie found the old paperwork on the desert land and placed it neatly on the desk next to the white pad and the pencil. Laid everything out for their meeting and said a special prayer of thanks for Mr. Bautzer – $8,000, wow!

The next morning, Mr. Bautzer flew to Las Vegas with his client and the $38,000, which he decided to bring in cash, just in case Maggie wanted to negotiate for more. The sight of those 380 $100 bills was enough to get her signature on the deed. The widow Folsom was more eager to sell the desert land than Mr. Bautzer was in purchasing it.

It was a real quick deal. Lemonade, sure I'll have another one of those delicious sugar cookies, sign here, thank you,

Maggie, and THIS is yours, said Bautzer, as he handed over the package of 380 brand new $100 bills to her. She was expecting a check of some kind. Who carries around $38,000 in cash? But it was impressive. Maggie had no way of knowing that Bautzer and his client did everything in cash. The client was Morris Sedway, one of Ben (don't call me Bugsy) Siegel's men.

Moe Sedway, known as Little Moey, sold the property to Billy Wilkerson. Billy owned two hot Hollywood nightclubs, Ciro's and LaRue's, and the *Hollywood Reporter*, the movie industry newspaper.

Billy held the Folsom Cottage property through the weekend, and then sold half of it to the Nevada Projects Corporation, Benjamin Siegel, President. The Folsom cottages sat on the land where the Flamingo Hotel was going to be built.

Nov. 24, 1945: George Raft had a beautiful home up on Coldwater Canyon near Los Angeles. Ben arranged for a large dinner at Raft's home, filled with prospective investors. Ben was going to get his Flamingo Hotel off the ground at last.

Siegel also met with Del Webb, who was going to build the Flamingo; the architect; and the construction company. Three days of pouring over the blueprints – and they finally had their plans.

The working number that Ben had in his head was $1 million for the project. A million dollars would be needed to build Ben Siegel's Flamingo Club. (The earliest references to the Flamingo Hotel, in the newspaper articles of 1944 and 1945, referred to it as the Club. It became the Flamingo Hotel for licensing purposes in late 1945.)

The Nevada Projects Corporation was involved with only one project – to build the Flamingo Club in Las Vegas.

SHAREHOLDERS IN THE NEVADA PROJECTS CORPORATION - AND THEIR HOLDINGS:

Ben Siegel: 195 shares

Charlie Ross, Phoenix banker: 100 shares

Allen Block: 10 shares

Billy Wilkerson, Ben's working partner: 125 shares

Solly Solloway, married to Ben's sister: 20 shares

Hy Abrams: 22.5 shares

Joe Ross, Ben's Beverly Hills attorney: 45 shares

Sam Rothberg, co-owner of American Distillers (Peoria, IL): 122 shares

Harry Rothberg, co-owner of American Distillers (Peoria, IL): 122 shares

Allen Smiley, friend of Ben's: 15 shares

Louis Pokross, front for 15 NY Mobsters: unknown number of shares

Morris Rosen, front for Frank Costello: 100 shares

Meyer Lansky: 100 shares

The same day the ground was broken for the Flamingo, Ben Siegel's wife, Esta, established residency at a guest ranch just outside Reno, Nevada.

Esta Siegel had to be a Nevada resident for six weeks before she could file for an uncontested divorce, and she wanted to be as far away from Ben as she could.

In 1931 the Nevada legislature passed a series of measures that helped insulate the state from effects of the Depression. These included legal gambling, instant weddings and quick divorces, and legalized prostitution.

It was an amicable settlement. Their two daughters would remain with Esta. Ben would pay for their schooling and expenses until they were married – $350 per week plus school tuition.

Esta would get the house that Ben purchased at 200 Delfern Drive in Hollywood, their New York apartment, Ben's Cadillac, and $600 per week alimony for the rest of her life.

This was 1945 – postwar 1945 – and building materials were very hard to come by. This was not the case for the Nevada Projects Corporation.

With the help of his partner, Billy Wilkerson, Siegel obtained lumber and pipe right from the movie studios. Wilkerson applied pressure to his friends in the studios, and before long, trucks from Culver City and Hollywood were crossing the desert loaded with lumber and pipe heading for the Flamingo Club building site.

Ben imported expensive marble and decorative woods for the Flamingo's lobby through the Mexican black market. Ben was big in the drug trade in Mexico, and his partners supplied the rare building materials he wanted for the Flamingo's lobby.

One of Siegel's best friends was Pat McCarran, US Senator from the great state of Nevada. McCarran reprioritized the building needs list for projects going on in southern Nevada. They were reprioritized so that Ben and the Nevada Projects Corporation could receive the copper fixtures and tiling they needed to get the Flamingo up and running by Christmas 1946.

This wasn't the way to make friends in southern Nevada. Protest meetings were held in Las Vegas and Boulder City by the VFW and the Elks. Their members were finding that they couldn't get any of the fixtures and pipes needed for their projects. All the building material seemed to be going to "that Gangster, Bugsy Siegel's joint, the Flamingo!"

While the Flamingo Club was being built, Ben and his girlfriend, Virginia Hill, were living down the road at the Last Frontier, Suite 401.

Each morning Ben would drive down to the Flamingo worksite and sign for the morning deliveries. He wanted to be totally involved in the Flamingo construction, but he didn't understand the construction business. During the day many of those deliveries would disappear out the back gate. The next day, the same items would be resold to Ben and the Flamingo. One truckload of lumber looks pretty much the same as every other truckload of lumber, right?

Ben's lack of business acumen mixed with his volatile personality ultimately resulted in the Flamingo being nowhere near ready by Christmas 1946.

Siegel had three Las Vegas managers: Moey Sedway, Davie Berman, and Solly Solloway, who was family. He was married to Ben's sister.

The properties that Ben already controlled in Las Vegas were the Northern Club – he had actually purchased controlling interest for $50,000 in 1944 – and the Frontier Turf Club. The horse book at the Golden Nugget was run by Ben's bodyguard, Fat Irish Green. Hymie Segal, another bodyguard, was running the horse book at the Las Vegas Club. Ben's racing wire, the Trans America Wire Service, operating out of Chicago and Los Angeles, was in place in every single horse parlor in Las Vegas.

A competitive racing wire, the Continental Wire Service based in Chicago, was run by a guy named James Regan. For a number of years there was open warfare between the two services. Even though 1946 wasn't a great year for Ben Siegel, his competitor in the wire business, James Regan, had a worse one.

During the Flamingo's grand opening, probably as a gift to Ben, someone in Chicago blasted Regan enough times with a shotgun to cut him in half.

Ben's chief lieutenants were Little Moey Sedway, who controlled many of Ben's Las Vegas ventures, plus his warehouse business in Los Angeles, and Gus Greenbaum, who was living in Phoenix and running the gambling business for Ben in Arizona.

In 1944, Ben and his friend Allen Smiley bought a warehouse in Cerritos, California. They called it the California Metals Company. They bought millions of dollars worth of stolen iron and other metals at very reasonable prices, and then resold them at a huge profit to large users, such as the US government. Moey Sedway was in charge of California Metals.

Sedway was beginning to make some decent money. However, he was getting too full of himself for Ben Siegel's liking. In a fit of rage and frustration, mostly aimed at the construction delays, Ben had Moey Sedway physically thrown out the front door of the Flamingo Hotel – and told him that he would be killed if he ever entered the Flamingo again.

After Ben Siegel was killed on June 20, 1947, Little Moey Sedway was one of the three men who walked into the Executive Offices of the Flamingo and took over. While Ben was alive, among other enterprises, Moe ran the racing wire in Las Vegas for Ben. Sedway was also a very competent manager of casino operations.

This surprised most of the Flamingo insiders, because Moey Sedway was Ben Siegel's go-to guy. If something needed doing, it was Moey who made sure it was done. If someone needed something from Ben, they had to clear it through Moey first!

But Moey Sedway had done what several Mobsters from around the country did – they reinvented themselves in Las Vegas and became respectable citizens.

Sedway was liked by almost everyone in the community. He got things done, to be sure, and he did them with style. He was an aldermen of Clark County (being paid $1 a year for his services). He was head of the United Jewish Appeal in Las Vegas. He was on the board of directors of the Clark County Library.

Then Moey went one step too far for Ben. He was asked to run for the Nevada State Assembly, and he said yes. Whether it was jealousy or not, Moey became persona non-grata in Ben Siegel's world.

Ben Siegel was another story. The merchants and the small casino owners downtown were aware that he wanted to take over Las Vegas. He already had points in every casino that had a horse book, and the handwriting was on the wall. Ben represented organized crime – and organized crime was something that Las Vegans didn't want.

When the Flamingo was ready for its opening, a whisper campaign was conducted all over Las Vegas. Dealers, deskmen, bellhops, valets, waitresses, and other hotel personnel were told to speak to guests and gamblers about staying away from "that gangster-ridden Flamingo…"

In Hollywood, one by one, stars like Spencer Tracy and Katharine Hepburn, who had told Ben that they'd love to come up to the Flamingo for the grand opening, came up with an excuse.

Clark Gable developed a head cold. Marlene Dietrich sprained her ankle. Gary Cooper said his mother was sick and he had to fly to Texas to see her. It seems everyone was pulling out of a commitment they'd made to show up at the grand opening.

The MGM movie stars were told by William Randolph Hearst (known to close friends as WR) that if they valued their careers, they'd stay out of the Flamingo. WR hated Ben Siegel because of Marion Davies. Hearst had information that Ben and Marion apparently had 30 or 40 one-night stands. This was just after Marion and "Daddy" (as she privately called WR) had stopped seeing one another.

Among his other enterprises, Ben also owned the Screen Extras Guild. He frequently would hold up studios for extortion money. "Pay me or the 'extras' who were on a shoot, and all belonged to the Screen Extras Guild, will walk off your set." And it happened lots of times. Hearst had a lot of friends in the movie business who hated Ben Siegel.

But the actors were not part of this group. Ben socialized with everyone in Hollywood. It was the studio heads who hated him – especially Hearst.

WR let it be known that no motion picture star, especially those with MGM, was to show his or her face at the Flamingo – or else!

Billy Wilkerson tried to promote the Flamingo among his movie-star patrons at Ciro's and LaRue's, but with little success. George Raft, however, did recruit a number of his friends to the grand opening at the Flamingo Hotel, an event starring Rose Marie and Jimmy Durante.

Numerous articles have been written about the disastrous opening night at the Flamingo. Though Ben had hired 12 uniformed guards to watch the patrons, many of the dealers were helping themselves to money. Luck was running against the house, and two rival casino owners, Tutor Scherer and

Beldon Katleman, both won nearly $100,000. The decks and the dice were running cold. George Raft was the only well-known loser that first night – it's said he dropped $75,000 at baccarat. But even with that win, the house was down nearly $200,000 on its first night.

The Flamingo Showroom was barely half filled. The great Jimmy Durante played to fewer than 80 people on opening night. Ben had leased three TWA Constellation jets to fly the rich and famous guests from the Los Angeles area to Las Vegas. But the weather kept the planes grounded.

The following night, Dec. 27, was much worse. Rose Marie played to fewer than 20 people, and Jimmy Durante said it was the smallest crowd he'd ever seen, even back to his saloon days. New Year's Eve was a little better – Lucille Ball and Desi Arnez were guests of the hotel, as was Georgie Jessel and Leo Carillo, better known as Pancho, the Cisco Kid's sidekick.

One of the problems was that the Flamingo Hotel wasn't really a hotel. It was a casino with a showroom and a coffee shop.

It had only 90 rooms and they were constantly being worked on. (Each of the rooms, per Ben Siegel's instructions, had its own private sewer system, and furnishings were running at nearly $11,000 per unit.) Without hotel rooms to keep the guests on your property, people will play for a while, but then head back up to the El Rancho or the Frontier where they had paid $5 for their room for the night. It was a long drive back to the Flamingo. *So how about if we play right here at the Last Frontier after dinner, Mildred?*

The Flamingo Hotel lost in the neighborhood of $700,000 during the 65 days it remained open. By the first of February, Ben had closed some areas of the casino, the Flamingo Showroom and the outside bar. The casino still had three blackjack tables, one craps table, and the slots on the east side of the casino.

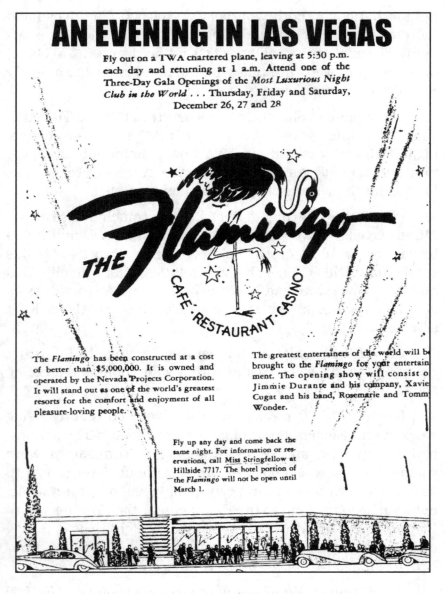

AN EVENING IN LAS VEGAS

Fly out on a TWA chartered plane, leaving at 5:30 p.m. each day and returning at 1 a.m. Attend one of the Three-Day Gala Openings of the *Most Luxurious Night Club in the World* . . . Thursday, Friday and Saturday, December 26, 27 and 28

THE *Flamingo*
CAFÉ · RESTAURANT · CASINO

The *Flamingo* has been constructed at a cost of better than $5,000,000. It is owned and operated by the Nevada Projects Corporation. It will stand out as one of the world's greatest resorts for the comfort and enjoyment of all pleasure-loving people.

The greatest entertainers of the world will be brought to the *Flamingo* for your entertainment. The opening show will consist of Jimmie Durante and his company, Xavier Cugat and his band, Rosemarie and Tommy Wonder.

Fly up any day and come back the same night. For information or reservations, call Miss Stringfellow at Hillside 7717. The hotel portion of the *Flamingo* will not be open until March 1.

This flyer was distributed in Beverly Hills and the Hollywood movie colony. A mailing was done to a list of VIPs and millionaires. Ben had three TWA planes chartered and waiting. Bad weather cancelled everything. None of the three planes took off.

Those gamblers and vacationers who wanted to see the Flamingo, and try their luck, were soon chased out by either the constant noise of hotel construction or the occasional very scary glimpse of Ben Siegel and his muscle – four bodyguards scowling at everything – walking through the casino.

Dealers would cower, hoping that Ben wouldn't stop at their table.

And then, on Feb. 6, 1947, Ben Siegel told his two publicists, Paul Price in Los Angeles, and Hank Greenspun in Las Vegas, to prepare press releases that the Flamingo Hotel was temporarily closing but would reopen as the Fabulous Flamingo within the month – billed as the World's Most Glamorous Hotel.

When Ben was upset, people who knew him would give him a very wide berth. Many believe his craziness was based on inherited insanity. He was a powder keg and, once he'd exploded, there wasn't much that could be done to calm him down.

Abe Schiller was the central figure in a public display of Siegel's volatile personality. I've read and heard many different versions of the incident, but I believe this is the way it happened.

As promised, within a month, on March 1, 1947, the Flamingo Hotel reopened as the Fabulous Flamingo. The grand reopening was held that Saturday morning.

There was no fanfare, but the hotel's front doors were opened by the Andrews Sisters – Patty, LaVerne, and Maxene. All three gals mingled with the guests, as did Joan Crawford and the Ritz Brothers.

There was free food and free drinks plus hot dogs and hamburgers out by the pool. People were encouraged to "bring the kiddies." One of the families showing up at the grand reopening was the Schillers – Abe, Doris, and their three kids.

Abe worked over at the El Rancho Vegas as entertainment director. He and the Missus wanted to see what was so fabulous about the Fabulous Flamingo. So the Schillers and their kids got into their swimsuits and drove in from Henderson to try out the Flamingo swimming pool and the free grub.

Ben had heard that Abe Schiller was encouraging his comedians, especially Joe E. Lewis, to joke about "that gangster up the road, Bugsy Siegel."

Normally Ben Siegel didn't carry a piece. He had three regular bodyguards who watched his every step, but Ben knew that his days were numbered and that there was a contract out on him. Besides his three regular guns, he hired one of the top button men in the country to become his fourth bodyguard – a monster named Hooky Rothman.

To be on the safe side, Ben was also packing a piece.

He and his entourage were walking by the pool when he saw Abe Schiller in a swimsuit. He exploded. He hated Schiller and anyone else who criticized his Flamingo. He ran over to Schiller, took out his gun and pistol-whipped Abe Schiller to the ground.

Then in front of Abe's wife and kids plus 200 or so Flamingo guests, Ben made Schiller crawl around the entire Flamingo pool. Ben was walking alongside him, kicking him and shooting over his head into the pool.

Hooky Rothman pulled out his piece and made damn sure no one stood up – or did anything else. The Flamingo guests and the Schiller family watched in horror as Abe, bleeding from his pistol-whipping, continued to crawl around the pool. Only then did Ben let another of his bodyguards, Fat Irish Green, take him inside. True story – it happened on March 1, 1947.

Regarding Ben's murder: He was 41 years old the evening he was shot. He had gone out to dinner with his friend and partner, Allen Smiley.

They went to Jacks on the Beach in Santa Monica. After dinner, Smiley and Ben drove to Virginia Hill's rented mansion at 810 North Linden Drive in Beverly Hills. Ben was on the couch reading the newspaper when someone fired a 30-caliber Army carbine rifle nine times through an outside window. Four bullets hit him. The first shot hit him in his eye; it was found on the fireplace hearth across the room.

Of the four hits, two were head shots and two were body shots. According to the police report of the shooting, the distance from the window to where Ben was sitting was "between 4 and 4.5 feet."

There are many theories on who killed Ben Siegel. It's generally agreed that his death sentence was voted on during the Havana Mafia Conference on Dec. 25, 1946, held on the penthouse roof of the Hotel Nacional.

Siegel was killed at about 10:40 p.m. Two hours later, at about midnight, Little Moey Sedway, Gus Greenbaum, and Morrie Rosen walked into the executive offices of the Flamingo as the new bosses.

Two days later, on June 22, 1947, there was a meeting held in the Executive Offices of the Flamingo. Attending the board of directors meeting were:

Joey Ross, Beverly Hills (an attorney representing Ben Siegel's interests)

Meyer Lansky, New York (de-facto chairman of the group)

Morris Rosen, New York and Las Vegas

Gus Greenbaum, Phoenix (ran Siegel's racing wire in Phoenix)

Moey Sedway, Las Vegas

Joe Epstein, Chicago (a Mob lawyer)

This meeting took place less than 36 hours after Ben's death. There has always been speculation that this group was already in Las Vegas when Ben was shot.

After discussing the Flamingo with Ben gone, Meyer Lansky

and the Flamingo board of directors took a break. They went downstairs to the Flamingo Sunrise Chuckwagon (all you can eat for only 99¢). Then they began interviewing two groups who wanted to become the new owners of the Flamingo.

Charlie Resnick, Sanford Adler, and Israel "Icepick Willie" Alderman were invited in to discuss the Flamingo. Their resumes:

Charlie Resnick – a 33 percent owner of the El Rancho Vegas in 1947

Sanford Adler – One of the owners and the president of the El Rancho Vegas

Israel "Icepick Willie" Alderman – from the twin cities of Minneapolis and St. Paul. It was said if you got Icepick Willie drunk enough, he loved to share his story about the "even dozen" guys who got in his way – and never lived to tell about it. His nickname came from the signature method of ending discussions known as the quick icepick lunge. It seems if you quickly jam an icepick into someone's ear, death is instantaneous and quiet. It looks like the person has just fallen asleep. After he left the Twin Cities, there were very few of these unsolved murders with that particular signature around any more.

Charlie, Sandy, and Icepick made their presentation, thanked Meyer for his time, and left. The next group making their bid for the Flamingo management included Davie Berman, a friend and assistant to Gus Greenbaum; Al Abrams, who ran one of the big legal brothels just outside Las Vegas; and Sam Diamond, a big-time bookmaker.

The decision that Meyer Lansky and the other Flamingo owners arrived at was for Sandy Adler to be their new front man – their man in the counting room.

The skim was, of course, the reason for the Mob's intense interest in the new ownership.

Sandy Adler bought the Fabulous Flamingo along with his partners, Charlie Resnick and James West. Icepick Willie only had a small piece of the ownership. Sandy and Charlie were both owners of the El Rancho at this time, and they were looking to diversify. The El Rancho Vegas was beginning to "slide" a little.

A final price of $3.9 million was agreed to. Sandy Adler and Charlie Resnick had to put down only $550,000 to secure the purchase.

The figure of $3.9 million is mentioned many times by the principals involved. However, the Nevada Tax Commission records show that Sandy Adler, Charlie Resnick, and James West paid only $3 million for the property.

Quoting United Press (U.P.) from the *Nevada State Journal:* "Costing almost $6,000,000 to build, the Flamingo has red-and-blue lighted bushes and a green pond, rugs thicker than a dealer's bankroll and more mirrors than a crazy house. Behind a fountain in the lobby were $7 to $30 rooms frequented by movie stars who liked the custom-made beds – six inches wider and six inches longer."

Sandy and Mrs. Adler moved into the owner's suite at the Flamingo on June 24, 1947. The owner's suite was formerly Ben's. It was the steel-lined penthouse on the third floor of the Oregon Building, the one always pictured behind the Flamingo swimming pool. The suite came with escape tunnels, buried floor safes, and all-bulletproof windows.

Sandy, Charlie, and Icepick – and Mrs. Sandy, Mrs. Charlie, and Mrs. Icepick – were enjoying the perks of being casino owners. Las Vegas in 1947 was a small town and the wives were able to socialize with the upper crust of Las Vegas society.

It meant when BMI – Basic Magnesium, Incorporated – was having one of their formal balls and dances at the country club, they were invited. Or when the Cashmans or the Squires were having couples over for dinner, they, too, got an invitation. Can you imagine how Mrs. Icepick Alderman felt when she received an invitation from Mrs. Tom Hull to attend afternoon tea at the Last Frontier to meet the guest of honor, Mrs. Eleanor Roosevelt? Mrs. Icepick had never met a first lady before, even an ex-first lady.

Sandy Adler was enjoying his new role as casino owner. More benefits than you could possibly imagine. All in all, it was a happy time for all the owners and their wives. But the real owners of the hotel, Meyer Lansky and the Chicago Outfit, weren't at all happy.

In the short time period since Ben Siegel was killed, the Flamingo still wasn't making money. Meyer's daily question was: "Who ever heard of a casino not making money?"

Sandy, Charlie, and Icepick knew the Flamingo wasn't making any money. It hadn't made any money since the day they took it over. One day in April 1948, Sandy Adler got a call from Jake Lansky, Meyer's brother.

Sandy: "Hello?"

Jake: "Sandy? This is Jake. Meyer sends his regards and says he wants for you to sell your interest in the Flamingo back to him. OK, Sandy?"

Sandy: "What? No way am I gonna sell out of the Flamingo. You tell Meyer that our luck's been running a little cold, but it's about to turn around."

Jake: "Oh! And Sandy? I was also told to tell you that you and your partners are going to have your throats cut and be buried out in the desert if you don't sell out right now. And Sandy? Give my best to the wife and kids."

Sandy Adler and the boys were very happy owning the Flamingo. They all agreed: "No way are we gonna let them kick us out. No way!"

Sandy and Charlie Resnick, along with junior partner Icepick, decided to talk to the "law." Actually, it was the

Nevada State Tax Commission who controlled casino licenses in the 1940s. They told the tax boys that they were being "elbowed out" by the Mob.

The meeting with the Tax Commission took place secretly in Carson City. The tax guys agreed with them – they shouldn't be kicked out of the Flamingo if they didn't want to go. And the Nevada Tax Commission was eager to assist them.

Very quickly it became public knowledge that the "supposed" ownership of the Fabulous Flamingo and the "real" ownership of the Fabulous Flamingo probably weren't one and the same.

And that was something that the Nevada Tax Commission found very interesting. (Even you and I know that when you take the Mob's money and get into bed with them, you're not supposed to go crying to the law about it. Unless you're ready to go into hiding, that is.)

And then Sandy made a mistake. After his trip to Carson City, he went back to the Flamingo. As he was walking past the reception desk in the lobby, he ran into Morrie Rosen and a couple of his gorillas. Rosen snarled at Adler and said: "We talk – now!" Sandy was quoted as telling Moe to "go fuck yourself." To the horror of guests in the Flamingo lobby, Adler was held up by two Mobsters while two others beat him unconscious.

Adler woke up 10 hours later in the hospital and came to his senses. He realized what he'd just done. He was released from the hospital, and Sandy and Mrs. Adler immediately drove to Beverly Hills. There Sandy stopped at the Beverly Hills Police Department and explained the entire situation to his friend Clint Anderson, Chief of Police. Chief Anderson told him it probably wouldn't be safe for him to move to Beverly Hills. So the Adlers drove to Reno and, with the help of their attorney, they sold 100 percent of their stock in the Flamingo Hotel.

The very next day, Gus Greenbaum was named president of the Flamingo.

Note: The day that Sandy Adler was selected to run the Flamingo, he hired Abe Schiller from the El Rancho Vegas to start work as the Flamingo's new publicity and advertising director. That same day, Hank Greenspun, Ben Siegel's long-time publicist, resigned his position as the Flamingo's publicity and advertising director.

Greenspun went to work for a small Las Vegas weekly newspaper, then joined Wilbur Clark for several years while the Desert Inn was in its planning stages. He eventually ended up at the *Las Vegas Sun*, working his way up to publisher.

From the day the Flamingo opened until the day that he was killed, the reign of Bugsy Siegel at the Flamingo was five months and 20 days.

THE HAVANA MAFIA CONFERENCE: THE VOTE TO KILL BUGSY

The Hotel Nacional de Cuba c:1946

Remember in the movie *Godfather II* when Hyman Roth is sitting outside on a large patio in Havana eating birthday cake? Michael Corleone and his brother Fredo were there, along with most of the heads of the Mafia families in the US.

This was a portrayal of the Havana Mafia Conference of Dec. 25, 1946, at the Hotel Nacional. If you take a close look at the photo of the hotel later in this chapter, you can get a good idea of the layout of the hotel.

The New York Mafia, at that time the strongest in the country, was designed to be run by the so-called Five Families. Until his imprisonment and subsequent exile, Charles "Lucky" Luciano was the number one man in America's Mafia. All national policy decisions and high-level problem resolutions were made by Luciano.

In 1946, Luciano had just been released from prison, spending most of his time at Danemora in upstate New York. He had been captured in Hot Springs, Arkansas, 10 years earlier during a vacation at Owney's Hot Springs Club. Despite heavy protection by Owney Madden, former owner of New York City's Cotton Club, the feds raided the place and got him without a shot being fired.

Tom Dewey was the guy who had been after Lucky for years. Luciano was the boss of all bosses (a term he would coin at this meeting). And Tom Dewey was certainly a politician. Lucky knew he was a big trophy for Dewey. Luciano was sentenced to 30 years at Danemora. They got him on abetting prostitution. Ninety counts – he was found guilty on 66 of them.

Nearly 10 years had passed and America had entered into World War II. Luciano had something that the US government and Thomas Dewey wanted very much. He had the New York and New Jersey dockyards under his complete control. The US government was afraid of sabotage, not so much from the Germans living in the US, many of whom were under surveillance, but from the Italians.

A deal was reached between Governor Dewey and Lucky Luciano. An accommodation between adversaries.

In exchange for keeping the New York docks free from saboteurs, Luciano would go free after the war ended. He would accept permanent exile to his hometown in Sicily.

Most Mafioso were extremely patriotic and approved Luciano's deal with Dewey. Both men kept their ends of the bargain.

After Luciano's deportation to Italy, he heard that his business interests in New York were being usurped by Albert Anastasia, and that it looked like there was going to be open warfare between the New York families. Charlie knew that Vito Genovese, who had come back from Italy to face a murder trial, was just acquitted. And with Luciano gone, Genovese was trying to take over his family. Frank Costello and Vito Genovese were at one another's throats. Costello also wanted to take over Luciano's family. And it did look as if it was going to result in a citywide Mob war.

Lansky reserved rooms at the Nacional for all of the participants. The Nacional was the only Havana hotel casino that Meyer owned in 1946. Luciano came in under an assumed name having spent two weeks traveling by boat skirting government officials.

In the immortal words of Hyman Roth, spoken on the patio of the Nacional, "This, Michael is what we need. A friendly government who knows how to do business."

Luciano was allowed to buy a small piece of the Nacional for $200,000. While he could have used his own money, it was supplied to him by the Mafia families who came down for this 1946 conference. The money was presented to Luciano in big fat envelopes, offered as Christmas gifts, from the Mafiosi attending the conference.

The Havana Mafia Conference's four primary agenda items:

One: New York's Five Families.

Now that Luciano was exiled and wasn't directly controlling New York, it was necessary for these men to decide how New York was going to be split up and operated. (Luciano was indeed controlling New York, but he was doing that in exile from Castelmarese, Sicily.)

Two: Reestablishing Control.

There was a lot of internal squabbling going on in 1946 in the Organization, as these men referred to the national syndicate. Beside the realignment of territories among the five New York families, there were jurisdictional disputes going on all over the country. Luciano was a very strong Mafia boss, and with him out of the picture, there were problems in many areas.

Luciano got an agreement from all these men, that he, Charles Luciano, would remain the final authority in the United States, even though he was in Sicily. Any major policy decisions had to clear him before action was taken. It was a logical thing to do; it reestablished much of the hierarchy and the peace, nationally. And then Charlie said, from now on, I'm Boss of all Bosses – *capo di tutti capi*.

Three: Narcotics.

This was an explosive issue. A tremendously profitable enterprise on the one hand and one that many of these men were opposed to. Luciano was the strongest voice of the antidrug group. With him now in exile, the bosses who wanted the income from drugs were prepared for an all-out fight.

Luciano again showed his leadership. He knew with him out of the country, a national policy allowing drugs or a national policy disallowing drugs was going to cause serious problems among the men here. He decided to make drugs a "local issue" – each family makes its own decision and lives with the consequences.

Four: The Bugsy Siegel Situation

Ben Siegel was not invited to the Mafia meeting. Luciano and Meyer Lansky knew that Ben was going to find out about this meeting, but with the Flamingo opening the exact same day as the meeting, he couldn't have come anyway.

Ben Siegel's Flamingo was about to open. The property was now about $5.5 million over budget – alarming for a project that started out at a mere $1.5 million. Siegel had misfigured costs time and time again, and he'd lost the trust of just about everyone.

Then, the men who controlled nearly all the organized crime in the US, learned that Siegel's mistress, Virginia Hill, did indeed have a numbered bank account in Zurich, Switzerland, that was growing steadily. She was banking skimmed construction funds. That meant that both of them, Ben and Virginia, were stealing the Organization's money.

Certainly there was some discussion about what to do. Ben had been around a long time. He'd grown up with Lucky and Meyer and Frank. But he'd been making too many mistakes, and now was probably stealing from them. The vote was taken. The decision made before the conference adjourned.

Six months later, June 20, 1947, Ben was killed in a violent and public way. Photos of him sitting on the couch with his right eye gone and all entry wounds visible appeared the next day in the *Los Angeles Times*. United Press (U.P.) picked up the story, and the next morning, June 21, this was what people were having with their morning coffee.

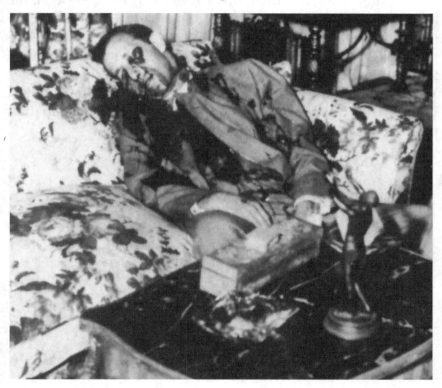

Ben Siegel. June 20, 1947, at 11:20 p.m.

The Fischetti brothers of Chicago, Charlie and Rocco, had been given the contract to take care of Bugsy. They were at the Nacional but were excused from the meeting to spend time with Frank Sinatra in his room.

Sinatra had a singing engagement in Miami during Christmas week, but left abruptly when Meyer extended an invitation to fly to Havana to entertain his "friends" at the Nacional. Sinatra literally cut his act short and flew to Havana that same night.

After the Havana Mafia meetings were over, Lucky Luciano decided that he'd prefer to stay in Havana than return to exile in Italy. He was forced to return to Italy, however, when the US found out that he was in Cuba.

On Jan. 1, 1959, when Fidel Castro took over in Cuba, the Nacional Hotel in Havana was "nationalized," as were all the other gambling casinos in Cuba. Nearly all of the Mob bosses had divested themselves of their gambling holdings there, with the exception of Santos Trafficante and Meyer Lansky. When both of them were forced to leave Cuba at the very last minute, they both lost a fortune when they had to give up their casinos to the Revolucion.

Attendees of the Havana Mafia Conference
Dec. 22-27, 1946

Anthony Accardo, age 40, Chicago, Ill.: Tony was called Joe Batters for his method of settling arguments. Although Tony took over the Chicago Outfit in later years, during 1946, the year of the conference, he was working for Paul "the Waiter" Ricca. Chicago Mob leaders Paul Ricca and Louis Campagna would probably have been in attendance, however, they were both serving prison time. Tony Accardo died on May 27, 1992.

Joe Adonis, age 44, Brooklyn, N.Y.: "Joey A" to his friends. Generally thought of as having been one of the four gunmen who shot "Joe the Boss" Masseria in a restaurant in Coney Island. The other three gunmen were believed to be Ben Siegel, Albert Anastasia, and Vito Genovese.

In 1956, Adonis voluntarily left the US. He was convicted two years earlier of being an unregistered alien. The feds found out his birthplace was Sicily, not New Jersey, as he told the court. He was arrested and convicted of perjury and was facing a two-year jail term when he voluntarily decided to go into exile. Joey A died Nov. 26, 1972.

Albert Anastasia, age 43, Brooklyn, N.Y.: For many years, Anastasia had the distinction of being the Best of the Best. The Number One hit man of Murder, Inc. Anastasia was probably personally responsible for hundreds of hits. He was best known for his trick of making trial witnesses disappear.

In 1955 there was a suit against him involving Charles Ferri, the man who built his house. Ferri was working on something at the Anastasia house and overheard a Mob-related phone conversation he shouldn't have heard. He agreed to testify at Anastasia's upcoming trial on tax evasion. Three weeks before the trial was set to begin, Ferri and Mrs. Ferri both disappeared from their home. Bloodstains were found in the house, but the Ferris were never found.

Then two other people who were going to testify against Anastasia, Benedicto and Vinnie Marci, were found dead, stuffed into the trunk of a car. And that was the end of the witness list against Anastasia. Case dismissed.

Three other cases against Anastasia had to be dismissed because witnesses disappeared or suddenly died. In one case four people who were scheduled to appear and testify against Anastasia were murdered. The remaining witnesses, though protected in police custody, changed their minds about testifying.

What probably led to his Mob-sanctioned hit was a culmination of just too many murders. Albert Anastasia was a made man in the Mafia, he was called "The Executioner" by his friends.

He was watching TV one night and saw a fellow named Willie Shuster being interviewed. Shuster was one of the people inside a bank that Willie Sutton had robbed. Shuster was called as a witness for the prosecution – he not only identified Willie Sutton as the bank robber, he went on to say that it was every American's duty to help law enforcement whenever possible.

Albert Anastasia screamed at the TV, yelling, "Hit that son-of-a-bitch." It didn't matter that to everyone Willie Shuster was kind of a hero. He was a nice, fresh-faced, clean cut young man who worked as a shoe salesman. He was newly married and had a great smile. "I don't give a damn! I said hit that son-of-a-bitch, I hate squealers."

The murder of Willie Shuster made everyone angry. Obviously, it was a Mob hit – it was a professional killing, and he'd testified against Willie Sutton. But he was just a kid, and he had such a nice looking young wife. "The Mafia just has to be stopped before they kill more clean cut, young shoe salesmen with their whole lives ahead of them!"

The killings had gone too far. Because Albert Anastasia

was a Mob boss, the National Council had to approve it. Which they did, on one quick vote. Albert Anastasia was kill crazy, and they were all going to be caught up in it. The police and the feds were already exerting far more pressure on the Mob than ever before. It was The Executioner's time.

It happened at the barber shop at the Park Sheraton Hotel. Anastasia showed up for his weekly appointment, his bodyguard went to park the car in the lot across the street – and then the bodyguard decided to take a stroll or feed the pigeons or something, walking away from the barber shop.

Two gunmen entered the shop, signaled for the two barbers and the customer in the other chair to keep quiet – they held the long barrel of a gun up against their lips – shhh!

Anastasia had a towel wrapped around his face. They walked up and shot him twice. He jumped up and lunged toward who he thought were the two killers, and he was shot four more times in the back. Anastasia had lunged toward their reflections in the mirror in front of him. Albert Anastasia was killed Oct. 25, 1957.

Joseph Bonanno, age 41, New York: Leader of one of the five New York families. He had a home in Tucson, where he retired after his second heart attack. He turned the daily operations of his family over to subordinates. In 1965 he faked his own kidnapping to avoid testifying. His son Bill Bonanno took over many of his responsibilities. Joe Bonanno died May 11, 2002, at age 96.

Anthony Carfano, age 47, New York: Carfano was better known as Little Augie Paisano. His gambling interests were in Florida. He was shot to death in his car in Queens along with his date, Mrs. Janice Drake, a dancer. They were having dinner at a Manhattan restaurant when Little Augie received a phone call, and they both left. Police believe the assassin was hiding in the back seat of Little Augie's brand new 1959 Cadillac. Two shots each to the back of their heads. Little Augie was murdered Sept. 25, 1959.

Frank Costello, age 55, New York: Gambling background, including placing slot machines throughout New York State. Took over one of the Five Families that ruled New York when Lucky Luciano was jailed in 1936. Vito Genovese and Costello hated each other for decades. During those years, Costello was targeted by both Genovese and the police.

When the Tropicana in Las Vegas opened in 1957, Ben Jaffe, owner and president of the hotel, was fronting for Costello, who was the real owner of the Tropicana. Costello lived on Park Avenue in New York. In 1957, he was shot leaving his apartment building by a Genovese hitman. The wound was only superficial. But the police found incriminating notes in his suit jacket – an exact tabulation of the wins and losses for the first few days at the Tropicana Hotel. A lot of people at the Trop lost their jobs over that.

Costello was also called in front of the Senate Kefauver Committee on Organized Crime, and although he went to jail for it, on live television, after putting up with day after day of being hauled in front of the committee, Frank Costello drew the line. He waited for the TV cameras to pan around to him, and he told the Committee what he thought of them, and then he walked out. On live TV, the Godfather, Boss of all Bosses, Frank Costello showed the Senators what he thought of their investigation. Frank Costello died Feb. 18, 1973.

Morris Dalitz, age 48, Las Vegas: When Wilbur Clark ran out of money building the Desert Inn, Moe Dalitz and his partners from the old Mayfield Road Gang in Cleveland purchased 66 percent of the Desert Inn. Over the next 40 years, Dalitz became the most powerful man in Las Vegas.

With loans from the Teamsters, Dalitz and his partners Allard Roen and Merv Adelson built the Sunrise Hospital in 1959. They also built the Las Vegas Country Club, the Boulevard Mall, and a golf course.

Moe was always known for his charitable contributions. He won many civic awards in Las Vegas and gave back as much to Las Vegas as he got. He lived the Mobster's dream, to get to Las Vegas and reinvent himself – and become a fabulous success.

He was a quiet, reserved person – unless you got on his wrong side. His smile was genuinely disarming, and most people forgot that you don't become a Las Vegas multi-millionaire and president of two casinos because you have a nice smile. He also had the reputation of carrying through on his threats.

There is a rather famous story about Moe Dalitz and Sonny Liston. Coincidentally, Dalitz and Sonny Liston were in the bar at the Beverly Rodeo Hotel at the same time. And Liston was drunk. He approached Dalitz and began telling Dalitz that he "ain't such a big Las Vegas tough guy away from Las Vegas." Moe Dalitz was 65 years old and was rather slight, Sonny Liston was a monster. Everyone who ever met Sonny Liston was awestruck by the size of the man's hands. They were nearly twice the size of normal hands. And Liston was mean.

He raised one of those hands to hit Dalitz, and Moe took a step toward him. Looking him straight in the eye, Dalitz snarled: "If you hit me, nigger, you'd better kill me. Because if you don't, I'm going to pick myself up off the floor and make a phone call. And very slowly, you'll die tonight!"

The stunned Liston thought better of what he was about to do, shuffled back to his room at the Beverly Rodeo, packed his bags and checked out of the hotel. Most people thought of it as a TKO for Dalitz. Moe Dalitz died Sept. 1, 1989.

Charles Fischetti, age 45, Chicago: The Fischetti brothers were first cousins of Al Capone. (Capone was 90 miles away on Palm Island. He had been released from prison, dying of advanced venereal disease.) The contract to hit Bugsy was given to Charlie. As no one was killed in Las Vegas, however, the decision was made to wait until Bugsy left Las Vegas. Because the killing was going to be done in Los

Angeles, Jack Dragna, Mafia boss in LA, was actually given the hit. Charlie Fischetti died April 11, 1951.

Rocco Fischetti, age 43, Chicago: Rocco, who was also called Trigger Finger, had just flown down to Havana from Miami with his brother Charlie. They were both escorting Frank Sinatra to the Nacional, where he was going to do one performance just for the boys. Rocco Fischetti died July 6, 1964.

Vito Genovese, age 49, New York: He became involved in the Lower East Side multiethnic gangs that also produced Charlie Luciano and Meyer Lansky. An assassination attempt on Costello in 1957 has been traced to a Genovese gunman. Genovese allegedly had called the ill-fated Mafia convention in Apalachin, N.Y., on Nov. 14, 1957. Police raided that conference, arresting everyone in sight. Genovese was convicted on narcotics trafficking charges in 1959 and earned a 15-year sentence. He continued to run family matters from behind bars through acting bosses like Tommy Eboli. Genovese died Feb. 11, 1969.

Phil Kastel, age 52, New Orleans: "Dandy" Phil as he was known, started off in New Jersey. He was very successful with the Mob there, and he was sent to New Orleans in the 1930s to work with Governor Long setting up slot machines all over the state. Both he and Huey Long made a lot of money on those slot machines.

Phil was one of the original owners of the Tropicana. He was responsible for overseeing its construction. It's said his wife who put herself in charge of things like interior decorating and building redesign single handedly cost the Tropicana over $1 million in cost overruns. Dandy Phil Kastel committed suicide Aug. 16, 1962.

Meyer Lansky, age 44, Miami: Lansky was the financial brains behind the National Syndicate. He was trusted by every family in the country and handled the split of profits to the penny, and everyone knew it. In later years, he was thought of as a Mob boss, even though he wasn't Italian. Meyer died Jan. 15, 1983.

Thomas Lucchese, age 46, New York: Also known as "Three Fingers Brown," Lucchese became affiliated with the Gaetano Reina crime family in the Bronx. Mob boss Reina was killed at the start of the Castelmarese War and was replaced by "Joe the Boss" Masseria. Thomas Lucchese defected to the Castelmarese side led by Salvatore Maranzano. Lucchese died July 13, 1967.

Charles (Lucky) Luciano, age 49, Naples, Italy: Probably the strongest and smartest of the Mob bosses in the US. Head of the New York families, he was the driving force behind forming a National Syndicate in the US, and he was its leader. Deported to Italy right after World War II, he was in Havana to reestablish his leadership of the US Mafia. Lucky Luciano died Jan. 26, 1962.

Stephano Magaddino, age 55, Buffalo, N.Y.: Capo of the Buffalo New York Mob. Magaddino began his own crime kingdom in Buffalo and maintained close ties to the Brooklyn group. In 1931, first Masseria and then Maranzano were gunned down. Magaddino was invited to join the Mafia ruling commission created by Charlie Luciano at that time. Magaddino died July 19, 1974.

Giuseppe Magliocco, age 48, Brooklyn. N.Y.: Related to the Maggadino, Profaci, and Bonanno crime families. A member of the "conservative" wing of New York Mafiosi, he became a target of the rebellious Joey Gallo and was reportedly kidnapped by Gallo in 1960. He reappeared, gave no explanation, and continued working. Magliocco died Dec. 30, 1963.

Carlos Marcello, age 36, New Orleans: Involved in New Orleans gambling early on. Distributed pinball machines in the 1930s. In later years, he was in charge of casinos, particularly the Beverly Club, where he was partners with Frank Costello and Meyer Lansky. Marcello quickly became the most visible member of the Carolla Mob, when the Kefauver committee focused on him. Convicted on RICO violations, many people believed that he was involved in the plot to assassinate President Kennedy. Marcello hated the Kennedy family. Carlos died March 2, 1993.

Mike Miranda, age 50, New York: Mike was at the Havana Conference as a *consiglieri*, an advisor to Vito Genovese and his New York family. Mike was often thought to be one of the two gunmen involved in the Albert Anastasia hit. Mike died in 1973.

Willie Moretti, age 52, Newark, N.J.: Willie testified before the Senate Kefauver Committee in December 1950. It was obvious that his mind was beginning to falter, he was saying things to the Senate Committee that he shouldn't have been saying. Willie was shot to death on Oct. 4, 1951.

Giusseppe Profaci, age 50, Brooklyn, N.Y.: He became an underworld leader in Brooklyn and found himself on the winning side of the Castelmarese War in 1930-31. He was made the father of his own crime family in 1931 with Charlie Luciano's reorganization of the Mafia. Upon Profaci's death, Joe Magliocco took over the reins of the Profaci Family, and civil war with the Gallo group broke out. Joe Profaci died June 7, 1962.

Joseph "Doc" Stacher, age 41, Las Vegas: Doc Stacher during the Havana Conference of 1946 was underboss to Longie Zwillman in New Jersey. Doc would go on to have his own Mafia family in New Jersey. Word on the street has always been that Doc Stacher was the real owner of the Sands Hotel in Las Vegas. Doc died in March of 1977.

Santo Trafficante, age 32, Tampa, Fla.: Trafficante was Mob boss of Tampa, Florida. Trafficante took the leadership of the Tampa organization upon his father's (Santos) death in 1954. He was friendly with Meyer Lansky, Costello, and Albert Anastasia. When he died, he had been Mob boss of Tampa for nearly 30 years. Trafficante died March 17, 1987.

Abner Zwillman, age 47, West Orange, N.J.: Longy Zwillman was capo of the New Jersey syndicate. He was responsible for the Jersey docks, but he had just met with Meyer Lansky and was told that with Lucky Luciano now in exile, he, Longy Zwillman, was going to have New Jersey and the New York ship terminals under his jurisdiction.

During the 1930s, Longy used to visit Havana with his girlfriend, beautiful movie star Jean Harlow. The Nacional was the classiest hotel in the Caribbean for many years.

In 1959, just before a subpoenaed visit to a Senate Subcommittee on Organized Crime, Longy apparently decided to commit suicide. At least, that's what the official New Jersey State Police report said. The fact that he was found hanging from a rafter in the basement of his West Orange mansion, with his hands tied behind his back, didn't seem to bother the Medical Examiner at all. Neither did the fact that after Longy Zwillman apparently hung himself, he decided to finish himself off by shooting himself twice in the chest and once in the lower back. Longy Zwillman killed himself Feb. 27, 1959.

Looking back, one can say the Havana Mafia Conference was very successful.

Jean Harlow

Approximate room assignments for Havana Mafia Conference, Dec. 25, 1946

FAT IRISH GREEN

Many people believe that Ben Siegel came to Vegas in 1946, just in time to build the Flamingo. He really came to Las Vegas in February of 1941, the same time that the Nevada legislature voted to legalize horseracing results by wire.

Ben invested some of his own money, and lots of his partners' money, in some early Las Vegas ventures. He bought points in the Las Vegas Club and the Boulder Club and Golden Nugget downtown, sold for a profit, and decided he wanted to try his luck out on the Strip, what was then called Highway 91. So he bought a piece of the Last Frontier from Bill Moore, the manager and co-owner.

Ben had a very persuasive argument. Each of these properties needed the income that came from bets on horseracing. In the 1940s and early 1950s, horse parlors didn't belong to the hotels, they were leased space. The owners of the horse parlors paid rent to the hotel and also paid a percentage of the profit. Ben Siegel owned the Trans America Wire Service, which was a monopoly. So, if one of the resorts out on the Strip, or one of the casinos downtown wanted to add a horse parlor to its income, it also added Ben Siegel as a partner. And in adding Ben Siegel, they were adding Ben's partners, Meyer Lansky and Frank Costello.

By 1945, organized crime, in the forms of Meyer Lansky and Frank Costello had already staked their claims in Las Vegas, and were looking for financial partners.

When you look through the files of the Nevada Tax Commission, Marion Hicks who was a builder from Los Angeles; John Grayson, an architect; and JK (Kell) Houssels, a Las Vegas gambling insider, were listed as owners of the El Cortez. The gambling license was jointly in their three names; however, Meyer Lansky was the money and power behind the El Cortez.

Bugsy, of course, actually ran the horse book at the El Cortez. He owned 50 percent of every horse book downtown and had 33 percent of the book at the El Rancho Vegas and the Last Frontier.

The El Cortez was built "out in the country" almost two blocks from downtown.

This was because Bugsy controlled the wire, the lifeblood of the bookie business. A wire refers to either telegraph or telephone, and its near instantaneous information.

A horse runs at Pimlico Racetrack, and within a minute or two of the end of the race, the winner, runner up, and show horse would be known and announced over the loudspeakers of the horse books at the El Rancho, the Last Frontier, the El Cortez, and the other gambling houses in Las Vegas. Each of these horse books subscribed to Ben Siegel's Trans America Wire Service.

Fronting for Bugsy was his bodyguard Fat Irish Green. What a wonderful name for a Mobster. Fat Irish was Old School Mafia – bust a head, ask questions later – and he ran a very tight and very profitable book at the El Rancho Vegas for six months.

When Bugsy sold the El Cortez and began building the Flamingo, Fat Irish went with him. When Bugsy moved into the Last Frontier, suite 401, with his girlfriend, Virginia Hill, Fat Irish Green stayed in room 403. FBI agents were in room 303, wiretapping everything that went on in Bugsy's suite.

Because Bugsy trusted his bodyguard and companion, Fat Irish, one night Bugsy gave him a locked suitcase to hold for him, "just in case."

Ben Siegel was killed on June 20, 1947. Two weeks later, Fat Irish Green showed up at Meyer Lansky's New York office with a closed and still locked suitcase. Meyer opened it and out poured $300,000 in $100 bills.

Meyer had no idea that Bugsy had given Fat Irish the money to hold. By returning it, Fat Irish was rewarded by Meyer Lansky. He was told he would never have to work the rest of his life. Lansky told Fat Irish to move into the top floor of the El Cortez Hotel where he would be a guest of the hotel for the rest of his life. A lifetime comp! Free room, free food – a very sweet setup.

In 1946, when this photo was taken,
Bugsy Siegel owned the El Cortez.

Jumping ahead 17 years to 1963. Kell Houssels still had the El Cortez. Enter Jackie Gaughan, a bookmaker from Omaha, Nebraska. Gaughan wanted to buy the El Cortez. A deal was finally arrived at, and Jackie Gaughan started his empire in Las Vegas.

Three weeks later, while Gaughan was going over the books, he found that Penthouse 1 at the El Cortez was inhabited by one Fat Irish Green, and Fat Irish had not paid any room rent since 1947. Plus, Fat Irish was eating two big meals a day at the El Cortez restaurant and wasn't paying a cent there, either. He had eaten thousands of free meals since 1947.

Jackie went crazy. He ran to his office and called Kell Houssels at the Tropicana. "What kind of bull feathers is this? I'm going to have to feed Fat Irish and put him up for free? No way, Jose!" shouted Gaughan.

Houssels laughed and explained the deal that Meyer Lansky had set up years ago, and that Fat Irish Green came with the El Cortez. Jackie called his friend Benny Binion to ask a favor – could he take Bugsy Siegel's old bodyguard, Fat Irish Green, off his hands?

Apparently, Benny owed Jackie Gaughan a favor. Benny said he'd take him, but for meals only. And for the rest of Fat Irish Green's life, he kept his suite at the El Cortez and ate every day at Binion's Horseshoe.

Just goes to show you, sometimes, it does pay to be honest.

HELP! WE JUST LOST THE THUNDERBIRD

C liff Jones was an attorney in Las Vegas in the early 1940s. Most people knew him by his nickname "Big Juice," because it was a moniker he'd earned well. Big Juice was an early dealmaker in Las Vegas. He put people together: casino owners with bankers, bankers with Mobsters. He introduced people who wanted to do business – and he got a piece of every transaction he was involved in.

Marion Hicks was a Los Angeles real estate developer who enjoyed Las Vegas in the late 1930s. Marion was friendly with Kirk Kirkorian, who was starting a small air-charter service between Los Angeles and Las Vegas, and Hicks was present on many of the flights.

THUNDERBIRD OWNERS
Mr. & Mrs. Marion Hicks - Mr. & Mrs. Cliff Jones

Cliff Jones was Lt. Governor of Nevada while he was an owner of the Thunderbird.

In fact, Hicks liked Las Vegas so much, in 1941, he, Jones, architect John Grayson, and entrepreneur JK "Kell" Houssels pooled their money to build the El Cortez Hotel in downtown Las Vegas.

In the days before World War II, most of the Las Vegas hotels and casinos were owned by locals. They were all on Fremont Street, near the Greyhound depot, Union Pacific Railroad station, and two blocks from the red light district.

Instead of building on busy Fremont Street, Hicks and the boys decided to locate on undeveloped land, a few blocks away. "Let's build out-of-the-way, out in the country where it's nice and peaceful and quiet. The hotel can have nightly barbecues and not be bothered by the drunks going from one casino to the next bar."

Construction went well and came in under budget. In the days before the war, this was fairly easy to do. Boulder Dam was completed and many construction workers who worked on the dam decided to make Las Vegas their home, so there was a good labor pool. In addition, Hicks, the visible managing partner of the El Cortez, was an easy guy to work for. The complete construction of the hotel took only nine months, start to finish. The total construction cost was $245,000. The El Cortez was a successful, small casino with a nice, active horse book. There was a two-story garden terrace building behind the casino with 79 rooms and eight two-bedroom suites. A room at the El Cortez was $6.

Sometime in 1944 or the beginning of 1945, Hicks was approached by Ben Siegel who was representing his boss, Meyer Lansky. Siegel made Hicks a deal for the El Cortez. The agreed-upon price was $600,000. Siegel paid in cash. Hicks took the money and moved out of the El Cortez owner's suite. Since the original ownership group's investment was about $125,000, they made a tidy $475,000 profit in only four years.

Ben now owned about half of the El Cortez Hotel and completely owned the horse book. The El Cortez was showing a nice, modest profit, but three miles south of town, out on Highway 91, there was a hotel under construction, the Flamingo, with a sizable stake from Ben. With Ben and Meyer now venturing into the resort hotel business, they let it be known to casino owners and Mobsters around the country that the El Cortez was for sale.

Meanwhile, in Minneapolis, Davie and Charles "Chickie" Berman were experiencing a lot of local heat. As gamblers and club owners, they were being leaned on heavily, and they wanted to try somewhere with greener pastures and warmer winters. So Davie Berman flew to New York to meet with Meyer Lansky with the intent of buying the El Cortez. Meyer gave his permission for Davie to return to Las Vegas and negotiate with Siegel to purchase the hotel. As part of the deal, Lansky wanted a finder's fee of $160,000 – in cash and upfront. Davie Berman had expected this wrinkle and brought a suitcase full of cash with him. He paid Lansky the $160,000, thanked him for allowing him to buy the El Cortez, and headed back to Minneapolis.

There he met with his partners and, among them, raised $1.3 million in cash. The Minneapolis contingent was comprised of Davie; his brother Chickie; Davie Berman's best friend, Israel Alderman, better known as "Ice Pick Willie"; and Moey Sedway. Once they arrived in Las Vegas to consummate the deal, they checked into the El Cortez and were met by Ben Siegel's representative, Gus Greenbaum, who had come in from Phoenix for the meeting.

According to Susan Berman's book, *Memories of a Gangster's Daughter*, while Davie was downstairs in the owner's office negotiating with Greenbaum, his brother Chickie took the satchel with the entire $1.3 million and went looking for some action. Moey Sedway and his men found Chickie at a high-stakes craps game at the Las Vegas Club. By the time they could stop him, Chickie had already lost over $900,000.

Crestfallen, Davie and Chickie returned to Minneapolis. Davie Berman promised his partners that the original million three would be repaid, but he needed to borrow another million to meet his purchase obligation. Amazingly, Davie Berman was given the second million and flew back to Las Vegas. This time Chickie stayed back home in Minneapolis. The $1.3 million purchase was completed, and the ownership of the El Cortez changed hands.

Opening Night at the Thunderbird Hotel

For years, Guy McAfee worked as vice squad captain of the Los Angeles Police Department. Apparently, though this was only rumored, he made so much money from his police job that he was able to buy acres of land just south of Las Vegas, along Highway 91. The property, which years later would be filled by The Last Frontier, included the "91 Club" Casino that stood on the land. The Club was making McAfee a fair amount of money, so in 1946, it was no big surprise when McAfee was approached by Jones and Hicks who are said to have made him a proposition: "We have a proposition for you. We'd like to buy the land you got across from the El Rancho for a casino and hotel." A deal was struck, title to the land passed to Jones and Hicks, and construction of the Thunderbird Hotel began.

The Thunderbird was never much of a hotel. It opened with only 46 rooms and a nice, but modest casino. It took all the resources that Big Juice, Hicks, and their partners could come up with. To open the doors, their out-of-pocket was nearly $1.5 million. But they were able to cut some corners. Since Hicks was in the construction business in Los Angeles, he also got licensed in Nevada. They built the Thunderbird with Hicks as general contractor who had his own construction crew. There were several minority partners in the Thunderbird in 1948. These included Tutor Scherer, gambler, casino owner, and soon to be poet laureate of Nevada. (In the mid-to-late 1950s, *Fabulous Las Vegas* magazine routinely devoted a full page in every issue to

Tutor's poetry or prose.) Guy McAfee also had a small piece of the Thunderbird action.

It must be exciting when you can be in your own casino on opening night after all the months of planning and work, knowing the mortgage will soon be paid off. You're finally going to be able to stand in your own craps pit, behind one of the high tables, and watch all the players throwing their money at you as quickly as you can take it in. It didn't quite work out that way, however, on opening night, Sept. 2, 1948.

The new owners and their wives were dressed to the nines. The place was flowing with excitement. There used to be a tradition in Las Vegas that, when a new hotel opened, all the other casino owners would show up and give the place lots of action on the craps tables.

Two casino owners, Jake Katleman of the El Rancho Vegas and Farmer Paige, another Los Angeles gambler who moved to Las Vegas and opened the Pioneer Club, were there. They were playing at the same craps table and, between them, had two chip rails completely filled with purple and yellow chips. There was a lot of backslapping, free flowing drinks, noise, and excitement – and sweat rolling down the faces of Jones and Hicks. Big Juice was having trouble catching his breath as he watched Katleman and Paige, two of his friends and rival owners, make point after point on the table.

The two players finally left the craps table, spread some major tips among the dealers, and with two security guards escorting them, brought rack after rack of chips to the cashier's cage. The cashier, with the Thunderbird owners watching over his shoulder, counted the chips and announced the amount: $161,310! The total cash in the Thunderbird's cashier's cage, back-room safe, Big Juice's wallet, and some extra just-in-case money they hid away amounted to a little over $41,000. Damn! They were a few bucks short. And Katleman and Paige, although pretty nice guys, weren't going to say, "Hey, don't worry about the hundred and sixty thou. That was just for fun." They wanted their money.

Early photo of the Thunderbird Hotel.

Big Juice and Marion told Jake and Farmer to come to the office. Marion asked if they could have two days to pay up the "one sixty large." Jake Katleman, unlike his nephew, Beldon, who owned the El Rancho Vegas a few years later and was a miserable character, said, "Sure, we'll see you Thursday for dinner and pick up the money then." After Jake and Farmer left, Big Juice and Marion sat staring at each other. Unbelievable. They had just lost the Thunderbird.

Meyer's Brother Jake

Neither Big Juice nor Marion were kids, they knew where that kind of money could be found. The Mob not only had funds readily available, but thought Las Vegas was a true blue-chip investment. So Hicks called a friend of his, George Sadlo, from Texas. Sadlo was well connected with Meyer Lansky. Hicks explained the problem and asked Sadlo if he'd contact Meyer to tell him that they needed $160 Large. Of course, they would be willing to talk to Meyer about a partnership.

Meyer was already deeply involved in the Flamingo, and the hotel and casino, under the expert guidance of Gus Greenbaum, was making money hand-over-fist for the Chicago Outfit, plus all the other people who had their hands in the Flamingo's financial pie. When George Sadlo called Lansky that night in September 1948, Meyer was living on the top floor of the Hotel Nacional in Havana and a deal was put together over the phone.

In exchange for a still-unknown percentage in the Thunderbird, Lansky would have $160,000 in cash delivered to Big Juice and Marion's offices the next day.

In addition to his percentage in the Thunderbird, Meyer wanted a part of the skim, and, most importantly, for his brother, Jake, to have a job there. Nothing fancy, just something that would keep him out of trouble, pay him a legitimate wage, and allow him to wear a clean shirt to work each day.

The deal was agreed to and the $160 Large was delivered to the Thunderbird's offices. (Does this sound a little like the first *Godfather* movie when Fredo Corleone goes to Las Vegas to work for Moe Green?) The money was handed over to Katleman and Paige, and on Sept. 3, 1948, at about noon, the Thunderbird Hotel and Casino was owned by the Mob.

During the Kefauver Committee meetings held in Las Vegas less than two years after this arrangement was made, Cliff Jones was called as a witness. Jones was still lieutenant governor of Nevada at that time.

Because of testimony at these hearings, Jones' and Hicks' gambling licenses were revoked. It was something concerning Meyer Lansky and George Sadlo's hidden ownership in the hotel. Cliff Jones later admitted in court that his 50 percent ownership was pared down to 11 percent after the loan. The license revocation lasted less than a day. Friends of friends spoke to the Nevada Tax Commission guys, and Big Juice and Marion got their licenses back. But the Mob was now in the Thunderbird to stay.

And Jake Lansky, Meyer's brother had a new job. When the guys got hungry, Jake was the one they sent out for Danish and coffee. And he nearly always remembered to get it and bring it back. Jake was the kind of man who was very lucky to have a good brother like Meyer. Meyer took care of Jake the way you're supposed to when you're worth a few zillion dollars and have a brother who always means well, but somehow doesn't do things very well.

Starting back in the '20s, Meyer let Jake help him out in a number of his business ventures. No one laughed at Jake Lansky because he was Meyer's brother. Besides, Ben Siegel liked him, Tony Accardo liked him, Frank Costello liked him, and so did Santo Trafficante.

At one time, Meyer owned one of the two casinos at the Hotel Nacional in Havana, the so-called Casino International. Jake was casino manager there.

He had a business card that read:

Hotel Nacional de Cuba

Jacob "Jake" Lansky
Casino Manager

Two other men who worked for Meyer were also on the floor of the Casino International, Merle Jacobs and Edward Cellini, but neither of them had business cards saying he was the casino manager.

Merle Jacobs was in charge of the casino's money, and Eddie Cellini was in charge of everything else. Eddie took care of the dealers, pit bosses, customers and all the other mundane things necessary to keep a high-volume casino running well. On the other hand, the International's casino manager, Jake, made sure that customers who were playing got the right drinks that they ordered, that the bartenders showed up to work on time, and that the maintenance crew got the floors vacuumed each night. Jake carried out his casino manager job duties very well, and Meyer was quite happy that his brother had job security.

When Meyer sent his brother Jake to Vegas, to "watch over the family's interests," Jake brought his new, black, 1948 Cadillac Coupe DeVille, which had Illinois license plates. And every day, Jake proudly parked it in the Thunderbird's owner's parking place. It soon became obvious to the Las Vegas police and FBI, after a few months, that a car registered to Jake Lansky was being parked right out in the open. It wasn't hard to trace the license registration. Jake was living at the Thunderbird. This started the investigation which led to the discovery of hidden ownership, and the revocation of Big Juice and Hicks' gambling license. (If you see a vintage postcard from the Thunderbird, look at the car parked closest to the front door. That's Jake Lansky's Cadillac.)

Later, when Jake was "transferred" to the Sahara, he was specifically told not to park his still Illinois-registered Cadillac out front. As a matter of fact, it was suggested that he not even bring it to the hotel. Jake was given minor jobs around the hotel to keep him busy. The one he liked best was picking up VIPs who were visiting Vegas. He'd meet them at McCarran Airport and make sure they got safely to the Sahara.

He was a careful driver and seemed quite happy with his new duties. In his pocket he always carried business cards that read:

Sahara Hotel

Jacob "Jake" Lansky
Casino Manager

TWO DUMB TONYS

On the afternoon of June 13, 1951, a first happened in Las Vegas.

It involved two dumb guys named Tony – Tony Trombino and his buddy Tony Broncato. Both the Tonys were from Kansas City. Tough and dumb, and not afraid to do what had to be done, as long as they were told what that was.

Tony B. had an uncle who lived out in Hollywood. Norfio Brancanto. Uncle Norfio was not only in the Mob, he was a button man for the legendary Mickey Cohen. If Mickey told him to get rid of someone, that someone was gone. Tony B. was proud to say that Uncle Norfio worked for Mickey Cohen. And, in the Mob, it ain't what you know, it's who you know, *capice?*

One day, Uncle Norfio asked Cohen if it would be OK if he brought his nephew Tony out to Los Angeles. Maybe Mickey might have a job for him. Cohen said OK, bring him out, but "I ain't makin' no promises."

Uncle Norfio called Tony and invited him to LA.

Tony B. ran over to his friend Tony T.'s house, and told him about this great opportunity that just came up with Uncle Norfio. It would give them a chance to get out of Kansas City, where they had 24 felony arrests between them, and start over new.

Working for Mickey Cohen, in the Land of Sunshine, Marilyn Monroe, and sports cars. Life was really starting to take a turn for the better.

The finance company had taken Tony T's car some weeks ago, and they needed a way to get out to California. Sitting just outside Tony T's apartment was a 1941 Ford Coupe. It belonged to their landlady, Mrs. Harrison. Nice old lady. She had a bad habit of leaving her keys in the ignition.

So, on June 1, 1951, the two dumb Tonys packed up Mrs. Harrison's old Ford Coupe, and while she was sleeping, they headed west out of K.C. To a new life in Southern California, working for one of the top Mob guys in the country. A chance for a whole new life, all they had to do was to remember to think before doing anything dumb.

Just outside Colorado, they decided to stop over in Las Vegas and rob the Flamingo Hotel.

They planned the heist as they drove through Utah. First thing to do was to find a good place to lie low after the robbery, until things cooled off a little in Las Vegas. Someplace close. Chances are that after the robbery, some of the people at the Flamingo were going to recognize them afterward.

They checked into the Kit Carson Motel, just up the street from the Flamingo, under their real names, of course, but both of them were wearing disguises. Dumb Tony B. wore false plastic teeth when he checked in. The first thing the motel owner did after they got into their room was to call Sheriff Jones to tell his office about two guys who had just checked in with Missouri license plates, and one of them was wearing dime-store plastic teeth.

The Sheriff's office said they'd send someone around a little later to see what was going on.

The boys headed over to the Flamingo, just to case the joint. They decided that the easiest thing to rob there was the horse book, which was run by an old-time bookie named Hy Goldbaum.

Until the mid-1950s, the horse books were actually concessions leased by bookies from the casino. All the operating expenses, including the sports "wire" itself, were paid by the bookie. Without that wire, which gave race results, a horse book couldn't stay in business.

Ben Siegel and his sales staff had a persuasive argument with the legal bookies in Las Vegas. Ben had an absolute monopoly on the wire service provided to the horse books of Las Vegas. He represented the Trans America Wire Service back in the early 1940s, and he managed to make sure that the only competition, Continental Wire Service of Chicago, wasn't anywhere in Las Vegas. And it worked. By early 1942, every single horse book in Las Vegas subscribed to Trans-America. Siegel charged anywhere from $200 to $1,000 per week, per location.

The Flamingo just before the Two Dumb Tonys rob the casino. (Note: Tonys crouching behind the white Cadillac on left side of picture.)

A little explanation of a wire service: In the pre-war 1940s, most betting was done on horseracing. Let's say a horse named Panama is running in the second race at Belmont Raceway, and you place a $2 bet on that horse at the El Rancho Vegas horse book. Remember, this is 1941, and the bookie at the El Rancho Vegas needs to know who won the second race at Belmont, so he knows if he can keep your $2 or if he has to pay you.

Race tracks don't allow telephones, so the question becomes how are you going to find out how the second in

Belmont came out. By having a racewire, you were fed results that were no more than a minute old. Across the street from the Belmont racetrack was a man with a pair of binoculars. He was watching the tote board, and when the results were put up on the tote board, he'd give the results to the Trans-America Wire Service operator in Chicago. And the Trans-America company would "wire" those results to all the horse books across the country who subscribed to its service.

So within a minute or two of the end of the race, the results were out, and the bets were settled. Without that wire, there would be no horse book.

Gus Greenbaum

President of the Flamingo in 1951 when the two dumb Tonys decided to rob the horse book in the casino. Gus retired in 1955, but was brought back by the Chicago Outfit to save the just-opened Riviera.

So Ben Siegel had the wires in ... and now he went to Jake Katleman, owner of the El Rancho Vegas and Bill Kozloff at the newly opened Last Frontier and he told them what was what. Katleman and Kozloff weren't paying for the wire – the horse book was leased out. The bookie had to pay for it, and that was part of his operating expenses.

Meanwhile, the two dumb Tonys were walking around and around the Flamingo casino. They sat down for a while at a slot machine, not playing it, just sitting there and watching what was going on.

Hy Goldbaum was good at his job. He knew these guys were casing the joint; they were just so damn obvious about it. After their second trip into the book, he followed them outside to their car and got their license plate number.

After lunch, on June 13, 1951, the dumb Tonys, their driver, and a back-up man walked back into the Flamingo horse book. Behind the counter was a "lay-off room" where the cash was kept. They forced their way into the lay-off room with their guns out, took two bags of money totaling over $3,500, and walked out the back door.

The people involved in the ownership of the Flamingo, men like Tony Accardo, Meyer Lansky, Momo Giancana, most of the south Florida Mob bosses, and the on-site managers, Willie Alderman, both of the Berman brothers, and Gus Greenbaum, were incredulous that not only was their casino hit for $3,500, but it was done in the open – with guns drawn! A very, very stupid, and a very, very disrespectful thing to do.

A robbery like this had never before been attempted, and these very serious men wanted to make damn sure that everyone would understand that it would never happen again.

The two Tonys miraculously made it out of Las Vegas. However, everyone in Las Vegas knew who they were. The Flamingo ownership knew their names and that they probably were in Los Angeles. Which they were, working for Mickey Cohen.

Tony Brancato soon wore out his welcome. In the great autobiography of Mickey Cohen, *In My Own Words*, Mickey speaks about the two Tonys, and why he wanted them off his crew: "Them two Tonys began to muscle people and bulldoze people, things that was uncalled for in this part of the country."

However, Mickey Cohen had other, more pressing things on his plate in 1951. He was about to begin a prison term (which is another story).

Jimmy "the Weasel" Fratianno was a made man. He, like the two dumb Tonys, worked for the LA Mob. Born Aldiano Fratianno, Jimmy was the Mob's top hit man at the time. He may have been a weasel, but he knew how to set up a good hit.

Fratianno met with the Tonys and told the pair he would help them knock over a high-stakes poker game where the take might be as much as $40,000. "Sounds good to me, Jimmy," they both said in unison.

On Aug. 6, 1952, Fratianno and his backup guys met at Nick Licata's Five O'clock Club in LA. Licata had planned a party at the club that evening so they would have an alibi as to where they were. Two cars took off to meet Brancato and Trombino in Hollywood.

There was lots and lots of "overkill" involved in Jimmy Fratianno's handling of the two Tonys – a full clip was emptied into the head of each.

Jimmy "the Weasel" was arrested by the LAPD the next day at his brother's house. With the help of a prominent LA attorney, and a witness who decided that Jimmy "the Weasel" apparently wasn't the same "Weasel" she saw get out of his car in Hollywood and get into dumb Tony's car, Jimmy was released and the charges were dropped.

It wasn't until 1977 when Jimmy "the Weasel" turned state's evidence and joined the Federal Witness Protection Program that he revealed that he was the one who had killed both the dumb Tonys back in 1952.

No one stuck up the Fabulous Flamingo again. Sometimes, it just pays to advertise.

A CHECK SIGNED BY 3 LAS VEGAS LEGENDS

The check was written on July 7, 1953. Drawn on the General Account of Elranco, Inc., owners of the Hotel El Rancho Vegas. Signed by three Las Vegas Legends: Beldon Katleman and Carl Cohen and made out to, and endorsed by, Joe E. Lewis.

All three of these guys were involved in helping color Las Vegas history. And Las Vegas was good to all three of them.

Beldon Katleman made a fortune from Las Vegas, and most people who knew him said he never gave any of it back. He wasn't very well liked. And he made his fortune pretty much on the up-and-up. No skimming, no Mob connections, no broken kneecaps, just a totally unpleasant personality.

Beldon was a multi-millionaire, who was in Las Vegas society, but usually couldn't be trusted, and nearly always wasn't liked.

Up until the very end of Katleman in Vegas, like him or not, you had to say he made his money the old fashioned way: cutthroat, hard-nosed, a "me" first, second, and third attitude in his business practices, and maybe a little insurance arson thrown in at the end. Beldon would have made it on Wall Street today.

Tom Hull built the El Rancho Vegas and was the first owner. He was a very difficult guy to work for, and for the year and a half he had the hotel, there were eight hotel general managers.

Hull lived at another one of his hotels, the famous Hollywood Roosevelt. He owned seven hotels when the El Rancho Vegas was finished, and he was in touch with the managers of those hotels three or four times a day by telephone. With the El Rancho, he demanded an up-to-date accounting of the day's transactions, including the casino's cash position and winnings to the hour, the restaurant take, and room rentals.

The El Rancho Vegas manager would then give the boss an action plan that he was going to follow for the next three hours, until he called again. Hull sold out at the beginning of 1943.

One of the next owners of the ERV (El Rancho Vegas), was Joe Drown, Baron Hilton's front man. Hilton held onto the El Rancho Vegas for a year, sold it to Joe Kind, who in turn, sold it to Wilbur Clark. (I always wondered why Baron Hilton didn't rename the place The El Rancho Hilton.)

When Wilbur Clark left for Havana in 1946 to work in the casinos down there, he sold his piece of the ERV to Jake Katleman. This was a great decision as far as the employees were concerned. Jake Katleman was a nice guy, he treated everyone with respect, and people liked working for him.

The ERV flourished for four years, but then Jake died in a car accident. His nephew Beldon, a 29-year-old mathematics professor at UCLA, was asked by his aunt to come up to Las Vegas and manage the El Rancho Vegas. Also, he was needed to help watch over the 49 percent of the ERV stock that his aunt had. It only took him two years to acquire his aunt's shares in the ERV. He now was the largest single stockholder, and with Beldon Katleman now having majority ownership, people were actively seeking jobs elsewhere.

Beldon didn't have too much trouble buying out his partners. He wasn't the guy you wanted to have as a partner.

The ERV was the first hotel on the Los Angeles highway; you had to pass it driving east from Los Angeles.

It had a restaurant where the 99-cent Chuckwagon Buffet was very popular, a gas station, rooms for $5 a night, a casino, and a swimming pool 50 feet off the highway for all to see.

The bubble started to burst on the El Rancho Vegas in the fall of 1952 when Milton Prell opened the glamorous Sahara across the street. The gamblers could walk from the sawdust-covered casino floor at the El Rancho across the street to the

Sahara with the cocktail waitresses in waaaay too revealing costumes, flashing lights on the ceilings, and plush red and blue carpeting. "What to do?" This problem has faced many casino owners when gambling profits begin to slip.

The answer was simple. You hire the best damn casino manager you can buy. The casino manager is worth his weight in gold to an owner. The good ones were legends, like Philly Bader at the Desert Inn and the Trop, Moe Kleinman at the Stardust, Leo Lewis at the Aladdin, Johnny Drew and Chester Simms at the Flamingo, Sandy Waterman at Caesars; back in the days when a casino manager had the authority to send a plane for someone, or buy a Rolls Royce for a favorite client. He also had the authority to have someone dealing craps taken off his shift, brought into the back and have all 10 of his fingers broken, and then be driven seven or eight miles out into the desert and left there naked.

To quote one of the legends, Frank "Lefty" Rosenthal from his column in 1969: "To be a really good Casino Boss ... you can't trust no one! Not your Pit Bosses, certainly not your Dealers, the Shift Manager is OK if you watch him close ... and don't even start me on the customers."

The very best of the Casino Bosses was **Carl Cohen.** Carl arrived in Las Vegas sometime between 1942 and 1943. He started working in the Boulder Club, then the Las Vegas Club, dealing craps. A great stickman! A good manager of the craps pit. Carl was the pit boss at the Flamingo for just six months when he was approached by Beldon. "The El Rancho Vegas is in trouble, Carl. How's this sound? Come on over to El Rancho, and you're the Casino Boss and the General Manager. And you get 6 percent of Elranco, the operating company of the El Rancho."

Carl Cohen probably was very happy with his life. He was always a gambler, he knew numbers, he knew people, but he was never meant to be an owner – a Beldon Katelman. Carl was meant to be a casino boss. Just as everyone agreed that you never really wanted to turn your back on Katleman or let him "have something" on you, everyone agreed that Carl Cohen was a standup guy, his word was good, and he knew gambling. He was worth his weight in gold (and Carl weighed over 300 pounds)!

He moved over to the El Rancho and the casino began to pick up. He loved the job, but he hated working for Beldon. Crazy and psycho were the two most common descriptions of Katleman, a man who took pleasure in making people's lives miserable. Carl Cohen was making a good living, but hating his job more and more.

Then one day in 1953, Cohen was having lunch with Joey Adonis over at the Sands Coffee Shop. And Joey offered Carl the job of casino boss at the Sands. "I likes 'ya, Carl .. Youse can call me Joey A." Joey had controlling interest of the Sands in 1953, along with partners Frank Costello and Doc Stacher.

The Sands was Big Time and a perfect fit for Carl Cohen. The check (next page) was one of the last Carl signed at the ERV before moving to the Sands. From 1953 through 1967, Carl Cohen ran one of the tightest, best regulated casinos in Las Vegas.

Carl was known for landing the most famous punch in Las Vegas, outside a ring. It was the night he and Frank Sinatra had a fight in the Garden Terrace Coffee Shop at the Sands, and Carl busted Frank right in the mouth. Sinatra left the Sands that evening. Carl lasted a little while longer.

Eventually, Cohen moved over to Caesars as casino manager. And then Kirk Kirkorian offered him a great deal at the old MGM (now Bally's), and then Carl took over the giant casino in the new MGM Grand. Carl retired comfortably from the MGM Grand.

It is said that **Joe E. Lewis** never saw a cent – not one penny – of the paychecks made out to him for $6,500!

A lot of money. Even more if you consider the fact that each and every Friday, Joe E. Lewis got a check just like this for $6,500.

Lewis would go into Beldon Katleman's office, Katleman would turn the check around on his desk, so that it was facing Joe, Joe would endorse it, and then leave the office.

On Fridays, Joe usually went in to Belden's office to sign his check around noon. He'd go from Katleman's office, which was right between the casino and the security office, then go into the Opera House, right across the lobby, which was open for lunch.

He'd order his usual, the Number 2: French toast with powdered sugar, and two poached eggs with toast and orange marmalade, and coffee. He was always given only half a cup of coffee; he'd top it off with the Scotch out of the sterling silver flask in his pocket. That was the flask given to him by his friend and benefactor, Sophie Tucker.

Joe had a gambling problem. Well, it wouldn't be so much of a problem if, occasionally, a horse he bet on came in.

While he was eating the last of the French toast, he was figuring on the napkin: "I owe that son-of-a-bitch Katleman $1.2 million. If I keep working here, and keep signing my $6,500 a week paycheck over to him, I'll be out from under the s.o.b. in just a few years. Then I have to repay the money I owe over at the Flamingo and the Frontier. Never mind, I'll never get out from under this."

Joe E. Lewis was a comedian. He lived on the grounds of the El Rancho Vegas in bungalow 422. He worked nearly 48 weeks a year at the hotel as the master of ceremonies. He warmed up the crowd, introduced the headliner, who was often himself, and after the set was over, he'd sit in the bar, surrounded by fans, drinking himself to near death!

A very funny guy who gambled poorly and excessively, and drank everyone in Las Vegas under the table.

JOE E. LEWIS
Starring at
EL RANCHO VEGAS

"I hate whiskey, it's just something I do while I'm getting drunk!"

"I went on a diet, swore off eating and heavy drinking, and in 14 days, I lost two weeks!"

"You're not drunk if you can lie on the floor without holding on."

"I drink to forget I drink."

"I wake up at the crack of ice."

Listeners would fall over laughing. Joe E. Lewis had been a big-time comedian in Chicago. He knew every Mobster and worked all the Mob clubs in Chicago. Lewis was playing at the Green Mill, a nightclub on Chicago's North Side owned by Sam "Momo" Giancana, when Joe decided he wanted to perform somewhere else. He was offered a lot more money by one of the clubs on Rush Street. And he wanted to move over there.

This was 1927, and Joe was told by the manager, "Machine Gun" McGurn, (a fine name for a Mobster), that he'd just better stay where he was. But Joe left anyway, and two weeks later, upon answering the front door of his Gold Coast apartment, Lewis was pistol whipped, stabbed, and his throat was cut.

He survived, but fragments from the butt of a gun had to be removed from his brain, and it took him over a year to learn to speak again.

Two of the men arrested by the Chicago PD were later released when Joe E. Lewis apparently developed amnesia. He said that Momo Giancana and Machine Gun McGurn "absolutely did not in any way stab me."

During his recovery he was hired by his friend Sophie Tucker to be a back-up singer for her, although he couldn't sing a note! He was broke and needed the work, and Joe would've done the same thing for her.

When he recovered, he decided that he'd been in Chicago long enough. Joe's friend Milton Berle suggested that Joe might like Las Vegas. That's when Joe called Beldon Katleman, and became a six-time-a-year headliner. Everyone who works in the casinos knows that you're not supposed to gamble. Some don't heed that advice. Joe E. Lewis was one of them. Within six months, Joe was deeply in debt to the El Rancho. Katleman worked out the arrangement.

Lewis was given free room and board, a little spending money, and he served as master of ceremonies nightly in the showroom.

In the 1950s through the 1970s, all the owners of the Las Vegas casinos had memberships in the La Costa Golf Club just north of San Diego. There have always been rumors about La Costa being a Mob-run and financed club, but La Costa was where people like Milt Prell of the Aladdin and the Sahara could have a nice lunch and a round of golf with Morris Lansburg of the Flamingo.

Doc Bayley, owner of the Hacienda, met monthly with Ross Miller, owner of the Riviera. No one socialized with Beldon Katleman.

It seemed as if he went out of his way to alienate other casino owners, and Las Vegas was a pretty small town in the early years.

The El Rancho Vegas burned to the ground in 1960. Arson was not only suspected, it was reported by the Las Vegas Fire Marshal: "Probable cause of fire – intentional setting of fire in area behind kitchen storage. Accelerant probably used."

There are at least two plausible theories about the fire.

The First Theory: The El Rancho Vegas was not doing at all well in 1959 and 1960. Bills were going unpaid, entertainers were threatening suit against Elranco including Harry James, Betty Grable, Steve Lawrence, and the Will Mastin Trio.

The fire insurance policy was totally paid up to date through June 29, 1960. The fire occurred June 17, 1960. Very, very lucky timing. Additionally, Katleman filed insurance for $500,000 in lost cash which was burned up in the fire, although it was in his safe for safekeeping. Another damn shame!

The Second Theory: There was a real heavy in Las Vegas named Johnny Marshall. His real name was Marshall Caifano, and he was an enforcer for Chicago's interests in Las Vegas. He had absolutely no sense of humor. Mob lore credits him with over 50 hits. One night in May 1960, Johnny Marshall was at the El Rancho Vegas show. He drank too much and got rowdy. Katleman had his security men pick up Caifano and throw him into the parking lot. Well, Johnny Marshall had a reputation to uphold. How would it look if a Chicago hit man let it pass that he was thrown out on his keester? The El Rancho Vegas burned to the ground three weeks after the incident.

Guests at the El Rancho were not hurt, as they stayed in cottages dotted around the property. The night of the fire, Red Skelton was staying there and took some pictures of the fire, which became famous. Supposedly, the other hotel owners in Las Vegas met with Katleman and persuaded him to take his insurance money and get out of town. He never rebuilt, and he moved to Los Angeles 10 months later.

Likable or not, he was a good businessman. He took his cash that he made on the fire insurance and bought some property in Los Angeles. For those of you familiar with LA, think about Chavez Ravine, where the Dodgers play. Visualize the ballpark. Now picture the ballpark completely surrounded by that giant parking lot. Guess who owns the parking lot?

Let's see, 23,000 cars each paying $8 per home game, 81 home games per year, that comes to a couple of zillion dollars income per year, right? Beldon Katleman did all right for himself.

Carl Cohen did all right for himself, and Joe E. Lewis did all right, too.

The movie, *The Joker's Wild* is the Hollywood version of the life story of Joe E. Lewis. Joe's lifelong friend, Frank Sinatra, played Joe in the movie.

UNCLE MORRIE AND AUNT AUDREY'S LAS VEGAS VACATION

Blackjack Game. c: 1953
Note silver dollars used for betting.

Back in April of 1953, if you were "connected" and lived in Omaha, Nebraska, you stayed at the Flamingo.

In the case of my Uncle Morrie, he had a connection at the Flamingo – he knew Sam Ziegman. Sam was a big shot in Omaha; he owned three and a half points in the Flamingo. He lived in Omaha, and it was fairly common knowledge that Sam was somehow Mob-connected. Whether it was true or not wasn't as important as the fact that he really did own three and a half points of the Fabulous Flamingo.

Sam owned some bowling alleys in Omaha, and he partnered with both Bugsy Siegel and Meyer Lansky. They were partners in the Greyhound Racing Track and the Chez Paree nightclub casino, both of which were just across the Missouri River from Omaha in Council Bluffs, Iowa.

Uncle Morrie was in the liquor business, and he had Ziegman's bowling alley account. They bought all their beer from Morrie. Nothing under the table, no beer delivered to the back delivery dock at 3 a.m.; just a straightforward supplier of a business staple for Sam Ziegman, "Owner of the Flamingo," as he was known around Omaha.

The fact that he lived and worked in Omaha and was an owner-of-record only – and didn't have diddly to do with the day-to-day that went on at the Flamingo – didn't matter a hoot. Sam Ziegman was an owner, which gave my Uncle Morrie his connection to Las Vegas.

Back in 1953, a vacation to Las Vegas was not generally a spur-of-the-moment decision. If you lived in Omaha and you wanted to go to Las Vegas, you didn't consider the Last Frontier or the El Rancho. The Sahara and the Sands had just opened and not too much was known about either of them yet. (The Sands did heavy marketing in Texas, and the Sahara on the East Coast. Neither thought that Omaha was a market worth cultivating in their first year of operation.)

Uncle Morrie: "You want to go to Vegas, Audrey? I'll go down to Sam Ziegman's over lunch and tell him we want to go. Let's see what he can do for us."

If you were a gambler, Ziegman knew it. The bowling alley had a very active book going in the back room. Ziegman's partner in the book was Eddie Barrack. Ziegman and Barrack had one of the largest bookmaking operations in the country. They were "lay-off" bookies. They took bets from other bookies.

If you were like many working people in Omaha and you wanted to vacation in Las Vegas, you'd call Sam or wander into his bowling alley – he'd be happy to give you his business card. That business card could always be exchanged for a dinner on the house out there.

Sometimes Sam would say, "Instead of paying $7 per night for the rooms, I'll get them to charge you only $4.50 a night. I'll take care of it. Don't worry. And how about if I get you folks into a dinner show? On the house, of course."

Sam Ziegman was smart. Not only did he make sure you got a deal on your room, when you got there you'd find a fruit basket and a bottle of bourbon, "Compliments of Your Friends at the Flamingo." Back in the 1950s, Las Vegas hotels built customer loyalty with things like that.

In 1953, Gus Greenbaum was President of the Flamingo, and he spent over a million dollars on remodeling and expansion. The Champaign Tower, as the Flamingo called it, or The Silo, as everyone else in town called it, was finished in 1953.

The casino was run very efficiently by Ben Goffstein, who would go on to open the Four Queens downtown a decade later.

On the weekend of April 13-15, 1953, Uncle Morrie and Aunt Audrey were guests in the luxurious southwest wing of the Fabulous Flamingo.

Ziegman really did come through – he got them one of the nice rooms in the wing with the private pools. That night my uncle and aunt were going to see Marge and Gower Champion at the dinner show. My aunt brought her fanciest dress with the matching heels and the dressy bag, as well as the mink stole; Morrie brought his good blue suit. As much as he didn't like dressing up like this, he had to admit that knowing Sam Ziegman was worthwhile – they did have a real nice room.

One of the most feared Mob button men in the United States lived at the Flamingo in 1953. Aldiano Fratriano, who later earned the name Jimmy "the Weasel," lived in the southwest wing of the Flamingo. And Fratriano's apartment at the Flamingo was right next door to Uncle Morrie and Aunt Audrey's room.

Other neighbors included Murray "the Camel" Humphreys; Jackie Cerone from Chicago; and a suite was always held for Tony Accardo, known at the Flamingo as "Joe Batters." There were four or five other rooms and apartments in the southwest wing that were always occupied by members or friends of the Chicago Outfit.

Also having a suite in the southwest wing with the private pools was Bobby Goldwater. A holder of a Gold Flamingo Card, given to the biggest VIPs, he was co-owner of Goldwaters Department Store along with brother Barry. Goldwaters was opened inside the Desert Inn – and it gave the Goldwater brothers a legitimate business reason to fly up to Las Vegas frequently.

Tony Accardo (aka "Joe Batters")

Mob boss of the Chicago Outfit from the mid 1940s to the late 1950s. In 1956, Tony turned the Outfit over to Sam Giancana, though he took it back in 1966 when Giancana went into hiding to avoid prosecution.

Barry Goldwater, who was a Phoenix City Councilman in the early 1950s, had his own reputation as a heavy player in Las Vegas.

For years, he was comped at the Flamingo by his friend Gus Greenbaum. In 1955, when Gus moved over to the Riviera, the Goldwater brothers also moved to the Riv.

That evening, my uncle and aunt had a wonderful dinner. They loved the dancing and entertainment of Marge and Gower Champion. And, as was the tradition back then, the entertainers introduced celebrities who were sitting in the audience.

That night, Morrie and Audrey were sitting just three tables away from Sophie Tucker and her pianist, Ted Lewis. Sonja Henie, who was playing up the street at the Sahara, had stopped by; and Jack Benny, who was opening the following week at the Flamingo, was down in front.

Uncle Morrie and Aunt Audrey

After learning that their dinner had been "taken care of," Uncle Morrie left a nice big tip, and at about 2 a.m. they headed back into the casino to try their luck again.

When they got home, Uncle Morrie told his friends that he'd "about broken even" on the trip, but they both had a wonderful time in Las Vegas, all thanks to the Flamingo's owner, Sam Ziegman.

Uncle Morrie is now about 85, and he still is in the liquor business. And he still works five days a week! And when I go out to Las Vegas, he always asks, "When you get out there ... see if any of the girls remember me."

THE STORY OF MR. LUCKY, TONY CORNERO

L as Vegas has always had its share of interesting characters. Certainly none of the fun ones were what you could call "mainstream," and like everyone else who enjoys Las Vegas history, I have my own list of people whom I really like reading and writing about.

This is the story about Tony Cornero.

Tony Cornero owned the giant Stardust Hotel.
He died under mysterious circumstances
while playing craps at the Desert Inn.

When Tony was in his early 20s, he was involved in some enterprises that were just on the other side of the law. The 1920s was dominated by Prohibition, and Prohibition meant the opportunity for enterprising men like Cornero to make a lot of money. He smuggled whiskey in from Canada and smuggled rum in from Mexico (both the whiskey and the rum were top grade), and he sold them to the speakeasies in Southern California. By the time Cornero was 25, he had made $1 million. That's $1 million in 1927 money!

His specialty was unloading these "rumrunner" boats out beyond the three-mile limit, transferring the liquor onto his speedboats, and running them into the coves of the Southern California beaches – until he got caught. Tony went to prison, and while in prison, he did what a lot of smart convicts do – he kept his mouth shut and his ears open. And he listened to the fabulous stories about what was going on in Vegas. Tony knew that Las Vegas was his future.

In 1930, when he got out, Tony took his two brothers, Frank and Louis Stralla, to dinner and laid out a fabulous plan. (Tony's last name was Stralla, also – maybe he thought it sounded too Italian, so he went by Cornero.)

It was common knowledge that Nevada was playing around with different ideas of how to stay alive – this was 1930 – the beginning of the Great Depression.

Nevada Governor Fred Balzar and the state legislature were about to make gambling legal again. It had been legal until about 1903, and was about to be legalized statewide again. But there was a catch. The cities in Nevada, especially Reno and Las Vegas, were going to be allowed to set up their own regulations, not only regarding gambling, but also regarding prostitution.

Uncle Sam was well aware of what was going on in Nevada and was watching the state carefully. Herbert Hoover had that big dam project, named after himself, that was about to begin construction east of Las Vegas, and with all those thousands and thousands of men working on the dam, some rules had to be set up – for the men's own protection, of course.

Rule 1 - No Gambling and Rule 2 - No Women! (Well, not within easy reach anyway.)

So Boulder City was built with No Gambling and No Women. The Red Light District, Block 16, was within walking distance of downtown. It was bordered by First and Second Street between Ogden and Stewart. All the prostitutes in Las Vegas were supposed to work in the cathouses of Block 16.

From the big fancy whorehouses like the Arizona Club, to the rum joints with one back room, like the Lone Star, Block 16 was where the liquor and the girls could be found.

Tony had met two guys in prison who said they were well connected in Las Vegas politics, and with the help of the churches of Las Vegas and Uncle Sam and the Upstanding Citizens of Las Vegas, those two guys were going to get Block 16 closed down. "Run them women out of town!" (And straight to Tony's place.)

The corner of Fremont Street and Charleston Boulevard in Las Vegas is "out of town" – it's in Clark County, but not in Las Vegas City. And if Block 16 were closed down, where were those poor girls going to go? Where were those thousands of men who were working on the Hoover Dam supposed to find companionship?

With nothing but goodness in his heart, Tony Cornero took an option on a 30-acre piece of desert (way out on Fremont and Charleston) for $1 per acre. The owner set the purchase price at $10 per acre. If this Cornero fella' is dumb enough to buy the 30 acres of desert way out in the middle of nowhere, and pay me $10 an acre for it – well, I just hope his check is good.

And with gambling going to be legalized within the year (again, this is 1930), setting up some sort of business outside of Las Vegas City would mean you didn't have to be under the control of the Las Vegas City Council.

You didn't have to limit the number of slot machines you could have in one establishment, and you weren't limited in the number of 21 tables or faro-tables. If you wanted to open before noon, or stay open after 2 a.m., that's your business.

You're paying the help, you got a gambling license, out in the county; it's your money, you do what you like. No city council to have to be nice to.

One of Tony's nicknames was Tony the Hat. He wore a nice white 10-gallon hat – a felt one with a stickpin in it. Tony sat down with his brothers Frank and Louie and said, "Guys, here's the deal – we got about a hundred grand left from the rum and whiskey business, right? What I'm proposing is that we give the two guys I met in prison five grand so that they can grease the proper palms in Vegas and the state legislature. We buy the property out in the desert, build us a first-class hotel – at least 30 rooms – a first-class casino, a great restaurant, a wonderful bar. Heck, we'll even put in our own airstrip! Bring in movie stars!" (Sounds a little like Ben Siegel, doesn't it?)

The Meadows Casino (1931)

It cost Tony and his brothers $38,000 to build the Meadows Casino, and they built it for cash. And they did put in the landing strip. Sure enough, at the beginning of 1931, gambling was legalized in Nevada, and sure enough, their casino pulled in customers from all over town.

People got all dressed up to come on out to the Meadows Club and Casino. They had a top-flight dance band, Tony hired Jack Laughlin, big-time Broadway producer of "No, No, Nanette" to come out and live in Las Vegas. For $500 a week. An incredible salary in 1931 – Depression 1931 – Tony wanted to stack the deck in his favor – and hiring a big time Broadway name worked – Laughlin created the "Meadows Revue" – and the Revue sold out every night it played.

The booze Cornero served was top notch – after all, it was "imported" from Canada and Mexico. Most of the liquor being served in downtown Las Vegas was bottled close to downtown Las Vegas. Las Vegas society began hanging out at the bar at the Meadows.

But the Depression was not a good time to operate a hotel and casino – and the two cons who had promised Tony

Cornero that they'd get Block 16 closed never came through. According to the Las Vegas papers from January 1931, the two men "were spirited away in the dark of night by masked riders never to be heard from again!"

The first resort in Las Vegas, the Meadows Club and Casino was built in 1931, just outside city limits. Tony Cornero's first Las Vegas enterprise burned in 1931, and the LVFD wouldn't help...it was "outside the city."

Unfortunately, the 30 rooms, which were built at the same time as the casino, went pretty much empty. The society people of Las Vegas who were drinking, dancing, and gambling were driving home afterward, so the rooms were more often vacant then filled.

Two months after the Meadows opened, the Cornero brothers sold the hotel portion of the business to Alex Richmond, a Southern California hotel man. They kept ownership of the casino. Three months after Richmond took over the 30 hotel rooms, on Labor Day of 1931, a terrible fire broke out. Most likely, it was arson – and was meant to destroy the casino. But only the hotel burned – to the ground! Tony Cornero and his brothers weren't real popular with the powers-that-were in Las Vegas.

Upon investigation, it seems that although the Las Vegas Fire Department heard the Meadows was burning, they just didn't make the call. The Meadows wasn't in the city of Las Vegas. It was out there in the county, right?

The Corneros retained the casino until early 1932, but ended up closing it for good that very year.

The Boats

A wonderful cottage industry floated off the shores of Southern California in the early 1930s – luxury gambling ships.

Although this was during the early years of the Depression, there were still lots of moneyed people in Los Angeles, especially the movie people, the politicians, and the idle rich – and there was no place for these poor souls to gamble in 1933 Los Angeles.

The ships were anchored in what was called "Gamblers Row," outside the so-called "three mile limit" off Santa Monica and Long Beach. Motorboats called water taxis delivered gamblers to and from the ships – and it was done openly. The *LA Times* used to run big ads for the ships; you could hear radio ads encouraging people to "Take a Luxury Cruise to Nowhere."

Names like the SS Texas, and the SS Monte Carlo, and the SS Tango were all heavily advertised. On a Saturday night, you and the wife could get all gussied up, take a water taxi out of Long Beach Harbor or Santa Monica, and in 30 minutes you'd be on the SS Tango. Fare: 25 cents; return trip free.

A fabulous restaurant, great bar, two craps tables, blackjack, faro, one-arm bandits, a great horse parlor, and a nice poker room were waiting. And Tony Cornero, who like all good hustlers understood people, offered a challenge: a $100,000 reward to anyone who could show that any game on the Tango or any of his other gambling boats was rigged. Cornero made a fortune.

The owners of the boats were Johnny Roselli, Jack Dragna, and Tony Cornero. All Dragna had going for him was a scary last name. Although he was *capo* of the Los Angeles

Cosa Nostra, he mishandled his family so badly, it was referred to by "made guys" as the Mickey Mouse Mafia. (This was reported in many phone calls taped by the FBI.) Johnny Roselli was with the Chicago Outfit, Jack Dragna was affiliated with the LA Mob. Cornero was by himself — without Mob affiliation.

The Five Families of New York became aware of all the money being made by the gambling boats out there just 3.1 miles off Santa Monica. Never wanting to miss an opportunity, Meyer Lansky sent Ben Siegel out to Los Angeles to oversee the racing wire and to work out a deal with Jack Dragna to cut the New York Mob in on the action.

Right away, Ben developed a working relationship with Tony Cornero, who controlled the boats. They were so successful, Tony was more than willing to expand the business.

The SS Rex

Cornero bought the SS Rex, totally remodeled it, and opened it on May 5, 1938. His investment, rumored to be $600,000, was financed by Ben Siegel and George Raft. Bugsy wasn't liked by Jack Dragna of LA or Johnny Roselli of Chicago. Chicago had put in the initial venture capital to get the fleet going, and now New York comes in with Bugsy and wants to take over. (This was a precursor of this same situation that would happen in Las Vegas for the next 25 years.)

With Ben Siegel involved, competition wasn't friendly anymore. Boats were burned and owners were found washed up on Santa Monica beach.

Dragna then put out a contract on Cornero, but Tony lucked out. An up-and-coming young whippersnapper Attorney General of California by the name of Earl Warren didn't like gambling. State Attorneys General who want to become Governors know that highly publicized cases that

*Newspaper ads like this appeared all over
Southern California. Tony Cornero and his
partners also ran radio spots for the SS Rex.*

protect the public from the horrors of gambling boats only 3.1 miles off the coast of Santa Monica usually spell headlines – big, bold headlines and votes.

The state of California and Earl Warren found a technicality – a way around the "Three Mile Limit." It was the way the three miles were measured. The state of California refigured the starting point off the coastline and declared these ships to be in California water, and therefore illegal.

Warren and the LA Police and Sheriffs got aboard small Coast Guard crafts and made their way 3.1 miles out to sea – bent on arresting Tony Cornero and closing the SS Rex. A pitched sea battle began; the LA Cops vs. The SS Rex crew.

The battle never involved guns. Tony wouldn't allow the cops on the SS Rex. He and his crew kept them off with high-powered waterhoses. It worked for three days, then Tony and his crew gave up the SS Rex and surrendered to Earl Warren and the LA Police.

Tony Cornero was arrested and told reporters that he had to give up because they didn't have a barber aboard the Rex – and as he showed them when he turned around – he needed a haircut!

The SS Rex was seized and served admirably in WWII. It was re-christened the Star of Scotland and was sunk in the service of our country.

Wilbur Clark was one of the minor investors in both the SS Rex and the SS Tango. He had a total of 3 points in each. When the SS Rex was taken, Clark moved to Las Vegas and recouped his losses in the El Rancho Vegas in which he purchased majority ownership in 1944.

The SS Tango

"Tony Cornero's Floating Gambling Palace, The SS Tango, anchored just 3.1 miles off Long Beach, had more gambling tables than any casino in Las Vegas," according to *LIFE* magazine (1938).

That sentence always had my interest because in 1938 in Las Vegas:

THE BOULDER CLUB - had 6 Gaming Tables

THE LAS VEGAS CLUB - had 12 Gaming Tables

MONTE CARLO - had 5 Gaming Tables

NORTHERN CLUB - had 3 Gaming Tables

PAIR-O-DICE - had 4 Gaming Tables

RED WINDMILL - 2 Gaming Tables

That would make the SS Tango the largest casino in the US and within 3.2 miles off the US coast!

According to *LIFE* magazine, "Tony Cornero lost the SS Tango in a poker game." It always intrigued me, where was there a poker game large enough that Tony could call a bet with a boat worth maybe $4 million? If the profit on the Tango was $100,000 a month – that would make the ship and the casino aboard it worth what? Certainly in the $4-million range.

The SS Rex Casino (winter 1944)

Although the Meadows Casino had failed in 1932, Tony was ready to bet on Las Vegas again. He contacted his friend, the builder and owner of the Apache Hotel in Las Vegas, Orlando Silvangi. They struck a deal.

From the time the Apache Hotel opened in 1936, through about 1945, it was the classiest hotel in Las Vegas. It had the first elevator in town and first fully carpeted lobby. The Apache was a meeting place for the movers and shakers of early Las Vegas. This is where the bankers would meet for lunch. Howard Hughes used to take his lunch here – so did Kirk Kirkorian, when they were downtown.

The deal was that Tony would lease the 'Pache Casino (as it was called) from Orlando Silvangi, and he'd rename it the SS Rex – after his dearly departed gambling ship. The City Council of Las Vegas remembered Cornero well from the Meadows Casino, and from his very public front-page fights with the Attorney General, and by then Governor of California, Earl Warren. They didn't want any part of Cornero.

On Dec. 10, 1944, they voted "no" to his request for a gaming license by a 3-2 vote. However, two weeks later, someone must have spoken with a Las Vegas City Councilman named Coradetti; city records show that Coradetti changed his vote from a "no" to a "yes" – allowing the gambling license.

The land-based SS Rex lasted a little more than 21 weeks. For whatever reason, the gambling license was lifted, and the SS Rex Casino in the lower portion of the Apache Hotel was no more.

When the SS Rex Club in Las Vegas closed, again Tony and the Missus packed up the Cadillac and headed back to Beverly Hills. When Mexico passed a gambling bill in 1948, Cornero was already planning to invest his capital and gambling expertise in Mexico's Baja California. He was working with officials of the Mexican Government, acting as an unpaid consultant in their new venture into casino gambling, when someone rang his front door during dinner. Cornero answered the door to two gunmen and four bullets – all to the stomach.

It was a clear message. The Las Vegas casino owners didn't think the expertise that Tony had picked up in Las Vegas should be shared with our neighbors to the South, who were going to do their best to take business away from Las Vegas.

The Stardust Hotel (early 1950s)

It took Tony Cornero a year to recover from the gunshots – but he did – and once again, Tony and the Missus rented a U-Haul, loaded up the Caddy and headed out across the desert to Las Vegas. This time to go after the biggest dream that Tony ever had: to build the largest hotel and the largest casino in the world.

For a small amount down, Cornero bought a 40-acre piece of land on the Strip. However, that was all the money he had. Even in 1953, you had to put a couple hundred thousand down.

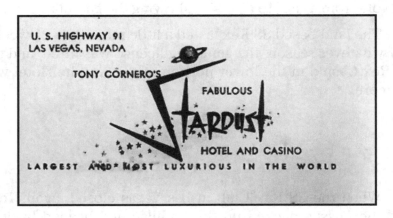

Now, he owned a piece of land and had a great idea for a hotel. What to do next? How about selling shares in the hotel? That'll raise money. (Have you seen the movie or Broadway show *The Producers?*) Well, before he could sell shares in the Starlight (that was the original "working" name, it changed to the Stardust later in 1954), he had to have those shares.

Tony filed with the Securities and Exchange Commission stating that he wanted to sell stock in his venture. Then he went to the printer and made up a whole bunch of stock certificates. As President and Chairman of the Board, he voted himself Stock Options – which he exercised immediately. The shares were issued for $10.01 each, and he himself bought 65,000 shares for 10 cents each. So he owned 51 percent of all the stock for a total investment of $6,500. The assets of the Starlight/Stardust at the time were 40 acres of land, valued at just over $500,000.

Easiest way to sell stock is just to sell it, right? So Tony and a group of salesmen who worked for him began "working the phones" selling shares in the "Biggest Hotel in the World – With the Biggest Casino in the World" for an initial price of $10.01 each. (Later, prices rose to meet the market demand.) Tony also took out newspaper ads around the country offering Starlight/Stardust stock for sale, and he ran radio advertisements in the Western states – and people started buying the stock.

Did I mention that the SEC had not approved this sale? Which meant that this stock wasn't registered.

All those sales that Tony and the boys made were valueless. Karat, Inc. (the operating company behind the Starlight/Stardust) had sold stock in the hotel without an underwriter. They were selling it themselves, why get an underwriter?

Meanwhile, construction had begun on the Stardust, and a lot of people were going to be out a lot of money. The state of Nevada ruled that those investors "instate" could keep their ownership; those outside the state lost all their money.

Next on Tony's list of "Things To Do While Building the Stardust" was getting a gaming license from the state. *("Damn," he must have thought. "I knew I forgot something.")* He was turned down by the Commission. He was not allowed to own a casino. Had to do with that silliness about him being a convicted felon and all.

So, here he was, with a giant casino, which had just begun to take shape, and he couldn't operate the thing. He asked his buddy Farmer Paige, owner of the Pioneer, if he'd like to take it over for him – lease the casino from him – on paper – for $150,000 a month. Paige said sure, but **he** wanted to run the joint. A basic sticking point between them.

The biggest problem in Las Vegas construction in 1955 was that there were far more projects going on than there were skilled workman available.

Union laborers were being paid twice union wages by Tony Cornero who was desperate to get the work done on the giant Stardust site. At the same time the Stardust was being built, the Riviera, the Dunes, the Hacienda, the Royal Nevada, and the New Frontier on the Strip; and the Fremont, the Lucky Strike, the Golden Gate downtown; plus the Moulin Rouge (in West Las Vegas) were all in various stage of construction – and they all needed experienced construction workers.

This photo taken by Mark Swain, Desert Inn photographer in 1954, was part of the Stardust prospectus by Tony Cornero. Most of the photos from this original prospectus are now part of the Conquest Collection.

Journeymen plumbers and masons and cement contractors and electricians were being offered staggering hourly wages to work on the various projects, and Cornero was bidding highest for their talent. His money began to run out fast.

In March 1955, Tony made the first of a number of presentations to Moe Dalitz and his partner, Meyer Lansky. He desperately needed money to finish the Stardust, and he was willing to take in United Hotels, the Desert Inn operating company as a full partner.

Cornero borrowed $1.25 million, which was the first of three loans Tony was going to ask for from Dalitz.

The second and third loans were soon to follow, and before he knew it, Cornero's dream, the Stardust Hotel, was being put up as collateral for loans. The Mayfield Road Gang, the Mob in Cleveland, was getting a bigger piece of it every day. Loans with United Hotels were now nearly $4.3 million.

Two weeks away from completion of the Stardust, Cornero was again out of money. He required an additional $800,000 to stock the hotel with cash required to open, and to pay the liquor and food suppliers for the initial stocking of the Stardust. "The bankroll for the cashier cages, and food and liquor needed to open – and that should finally do it. We won't need any more money," Tony explained at a meeting on July 31, 1955, at 9:30 a.m.

At 11:20 a.m. on July 31, 1955, Tony Cornero died.

There's always been speculation about his death, although the facts of his death were fairly straightforward. He was playing craps at the Desert Inn after meeting with Moe Dalitz. He was drinking his regular 7 & 7s. Tony was down $37,600 at the table, when, suddenly, he fell over dead.

Many historians and authors speculate that his death was caused by a heart attack brought on by Moe Dalitz. Tony, who was certainly a high roller, had been given the ultimate insult: moments before, he was presented with a $25 bill for his drinks, which blew his blood pressure through the roof – and brought on the heart attack.

From local newspaper stories:

- Tony Cornero dropped dead at approximately 11:20 a.m. at a craps table at the DI.

- His body was taken off the casino floor and brought into a casino host's office before the coroner or the sheriff was called.

- Two hours later – at about 1:15 p.m. – the Las Vegas Sheriff's department was called, and Tony Cornero's death was reported.

- The glass which Tony was drinking out of was washed. They could never find which glass he was actually using.

- No autopsy was performed. His body was sent by railroad to Los Angeles that night. Two days later, a coroner's jury in LA – again without the benefit of an autopsy – agreed with the doctor in Las Vegas that Tony died of natural causes, and he was buried.

The word on the street, of course, has always been that Cornero was poisoned. It was never proven.

The Stardust, which had been put up as collateral for the previous loans, now became the property of United Hotels.

Tony's brother, Louis Stralla, came in to complete the Stardust, but that became an impossible situation.

The day after Tony died, the Stardust construction site had a work stoppage. Donald Patterson, who was the general contractor, finally stopped working on the site, saying that the "jurisdictional disputes were just too much to deal with." The construction crew had not been paid last week, or this week. They were being told by the guys at Karat, Inc., the old owners, that the Stardust was now owned by United Hotels, and that the paychecks would get themselves straightened out soon. But they never did.

The giant Stardust, the world's largest hotel, with the world's largest casino, almost opened. Just as it was nearing completion, the Stardust property was fenced off, and no additional work was done for two more years.

More than 1,000 mourners attended Tony's funeral, including nearly all the casino owners from the Strip. Per his request, his favorite song, "The Wabash Cannonball" was sung.

Although Tony raised nearly $10 million in the 18 months before his death, through stock sales and loans, his bank account, which turned out to be all of Cornero's assets, had only $800 in it the day he died.

The actor Cary Grant played Tony Cornero in the 1943 movie *Mr. Lucky* co-starring Loraine Day. From October 1959 through September 1960, the TV show "Mr. Lucky" was also loosely based on Tony Cornero's life.

HISTORY AND MYSTERY
OF THE MOULIN ROUGE

B ack in September 2003, I had an item in my collection that I thought I'd offer on eBay. It was an autographed menu from the Moulin Rouge Hotel and Casino in Las Vegas.

It was autographed by Joe Louis, the ex-boxer, who was working in Las Vegas because he had to work, bad investments and all.

The casino owners in Las Vegas were very happy to use his celebrity status – he was recognizable and he was a nice guy, and people liked to have their picture taken with The Champ. So I had my menu from the MR (as it was called), autographed by The Champ, matted and framed, and I offered it on eBay. The autographed menu was an interesting item, but certainly not a rarity.

I decided to do a little investigating into what happened to that hotel/casino. What is interesting is that there was almost no information on why a hotel/casino that had become so popular, suddenly closed. One of the few books written about the MR was by Dick Taylor in 1995. It's called *Moulin Rouge – Hotel History*, published by Beehive Press, and that's just about all that's out there. It's as if the hotel didn't exist. Yet, putting together a few facts about that year, plus a lot of stories, one gets a general idea of what happened.

It was early in 1955. The Strip hotels were doing well. There was a lot of building going on. Smart money from all over the country was watching what was happening at the El Rancho Vegas and the Last Frontier and the Sahara and the Flamingo and the Sands.

Likable or not, the Mobsters who owned the casinos, and the casino owners who fronted for them, were a bright group of guys. These were money men; they understood gambling, and they understood gamblers.

The New Frontier: The new owners, Murray Randolph, Irv Leff, and Maury Friedman had just paid Jake Kozloff, Guy McAfee, and Beldon Katleman a lot of money to buy the New Frontier. Then, it cost them a few hundred thousand more to fine tune the place once it opened.

These very serious men and new hotel owners needed cash flow fast and didn't need no competition from no uppity you-know-whats like the owners of the Moulin Rouge.

The Royal Nevada: Sid Wyman was a casino executive at the Sands. He had points in the Sands, but he wanted to be a casino owner. Sid's partner, Al Moll, came from Missouri because of that damn Estes Kefauver and his damn Organized Crime Committee.

Moll had closed his Christmas accounts at the St. Louis bank, sold his interests in the casinos in Kentucky and Tennessee, and brought a lot of cash to the Land of Golden Opportunity. A place where a gambler could make a decent living, and do it legally.

It cost Al and Sid $5 million to get the doors of The Royal Nevada open. And these very serious men and new hotel owners needed cash flow fast. They didn't need no competition from no uppity you-know-whats like the owners of the Moulin Rouge.

The Riviera: The Riv had been open for three months, and it had lost money for three months. Tony Accardo, who was Mob boss of the Chicago Outfit, and the de-facto owner of the Riviera, also was a bright guy who knew gambling and gamblers. But he also knew that if your casino loses every single day for 90 days straight – probably it was more than just a run of bad luck. The Gensburg brothers and a number of other people were suspected by Tony Accardo of taking more than they should have been taking.

Tony Accardo told the team of Riviera owners to pack their bags, pick up some souvenir postcards, and be out of the hotel within 15 minutes.

Meanwhile, Gus Greenbaum, newly retired president of the Flamingo, had moved to Scottsdale. The owner of the Riviera, "Big Tuna" Tony Accardo, asked Gus to come to Vegas and save the hotel.

At first, Gus said no, but Marshall Caifano (Johnny Marshall in Vegas) who was the number one enforcer for the Chicago Outfit (he really liked blowtorches), was usually very persuasive, but Gus said he just wasn't going back to Las Vegas, period.

Four nights later, Gus's sister-in-law was murdered in her bed. Gus changed his mind. He brought his management group from the days he owned the Flamingo, but in order to purchase the Riviera, Gus had to raise some serious cash fast. He sold pieces of the Riv to his old group.

These managers weren't wealthy men. They had to mortgage homes and borrow anywhere they could to raise their stake, and they sure as beans didn't need no competition, especially from some uppity you-know-whats like the owners of the Moulin Rouge.

The Dunes: Stan Miller left a good job at the Sahara to buy into the brand new Dunes. Sid Wyman, Kewpie Rich, Butch Goldstein, Major Riddle, Bob Rice, and Howie Engel were licensed owners.

Morris Shenker, the attorney for the Mob, was also an owner, as was Ray Patriarca – the *capo* of the New England La Cosa Nostra.

All these men had spent a lot of time and a lot of money getting the Dunes open. Much of the money they put into it was borrowed. They had a lot riding on the success of the brand new Dunes Hotel and Country Club. And these very serious men and new hotel owners needed cash flow fast, and they didn't need no competition from no uppity you-know-whats like the owners of the Moulin Rouge.

At the same time, the **Fremont**, Doc Bayley's **Hacienda**, and the **Tropicana** were nearly finished. And then, in the midst of all this building, there was an economic downturn across the country. Las Vegas started getting fewer visitors. All these very serious men and new casino owners were getting worried about all the competition.

It was the middle of the 20th century, and most of the black entertainers in Las Vegas in the 1940s and early 1950s went to West Las Vegas to sleep and eat. West Las Vegas at that time was pretty bad. Muddy streets. Little plumbing, little electricity. That's where most of the black entertainers who worked in Las Vegas lived, as did the maids and the kitchen help. Even Sammy Davis, Jr., and his dad, Sammy, Sr., along with his uncle Will Mastin, stayed in the rooming houses in that poor section of town; there were laws back then about such things.

And then, in mid-May, 1955, the Moulin Rouge Hotel and Casino opened out on West Bonanza with 105 rooms. It was variously called the First Multiracial or Integrated or Cosmopolitan Hotel in Las Vegas. Blacks were welcome, Whites were welcome, even Benny Binion was welcome!

The two majority owners of the Moulin Rouge were Louis Rubin, who made his money from New York restaurants, and Al Bisno, a Los Angeles builder, both white.

The Rouge had a total of eight owners who bought partnership in the casino: George Altman, who became the casino boss, Al Childs, Will Schwartz, Larry Ouseley, Walter Zick, and Tom Foley. Tom was the hotel's attorney who was also licensed by the state of Nevada to operate the bar/tavern at the Rouge.

Joe Louis was the last of the "owners." In exchange for the Champ's services, Lou and Al gave Louis 2 points in the hotel. Some sources say that Joe was only an employee, but

LIFE magazine, which came out a month after the Rouge opened, referred to him as, "Former Heavyweight Boxing Champion Joe Louis, an owner and host of the New Moulin Rouge."

There were 17 additional investors, none of whom were licensed by the state, and as such, none of whom had to have their names published. Each point of the hotel prior to building cost $24,000, and you had to buy a minimum of 1 point to become a limited partner.

Hotel Personnel

Sonny Blackwell - General Manager (former Harlem Globetrotter)

Martin Black - Publicist of the Rouge

George Altman - Casino Manager (left his pit boss job at The Last Frontier for this job)

All the dealers at the Rouge were white. They were the only jobs at the hotels that were not filled by blacks. Prior to the Moulin Rouge, blacks couldn't deal or be involved in any casino games, so there were no experienced dealers to draw from.

Casino Personnel

Morry Deitch - Assistant Casino Manager (previously with the Golden Nugget)

Monk Schaefer - Swing Shift Pit Boss

Cliff Marshon - Dealer

Carl Walton - Dealer

John Achoff - Pit Boss

Joe Chariara - Pit Boss

Entertainment

Wally Ogle - Stage Manager

Benny Parson - first Orchestra Leader (4 months) until he was replaced by Les Brown who was there for the last two months of the Moulin Rouge's life

Security

There were 25 interracial security staff, all wearing the French Foreign Legion dress uniforms complete with plumed hats.

Merle Longnecker (Head of Security) - retired after 25 years as Inspector of Homicide with the Oakland, California, PD

Andy Rocknie "Rockie" - Assistant Security Chief - Retired State Senator from Wyoming, retired Pro Wrestler

---

May 1955 – The night the Moulin Rouge opened:

Liberace was playing at the Riviera.

Carmen Miranda was headlining at the New Frontier.

Louis Prima and Keely Smith were at the Sahara.

The Delta Rhythm Boys were featured at the Sands.

The Platters opened the Moulin Rouge.

Opening Night at the Moulin Rouge

The place was packed. It was attended by all the major newspapers, magazines, and the wire services. Martin Black, PR man for the Rouge, had arranged and paid for 70 news people to come in from the East Coast and the Midwest.

The first show at the Rouge was "Tropi-Can-Can," the largest chorus line in Las Vegas with 23 dancers. During much of 1954, the Moulin Rouge entertainment staff held open, and very well-publicized auditions all over the US looking for black dancers and chorus girls to dance on the line at the new hotel.

Local, state, and federal officials were all over the Rouge on opening night, including Mayor C.D. Baker of Las Vegas.

Advertisement in Las Vegas Magazine, 1955.
The Moulin Rouge was in business for only six months.

Some later entertainers to play at the Moulin Rouge were Harry Belafonte, Della Reese, Hines Hines and Dad (a very, very young Maurice and Gregory Hines and their dad), The Penguins (right before their big hit "Earth Angel"), Dinah

Washington, Lionel Hampton, Duke Ellington, Sammy Davis, Jr., with Sammy Davis, Sr., Will Mastin, and Ella Fitzgerald. She, like many of the black headliners, kept a two-room suite at the Rouge.

The Moulin Rouge had what was called a "Breakfast Show," at 1:30 a.m., and it attracted most of the entertainers from the Strip. After the second show was over at the Sands and the Sahara and the Silver Slipper, the entertainers, the singers, the showgirls and boys would head over to the Moulin Rouge to sit in on the jam sessions. The impromptu get-togethers quickly became popular.

A typical night at the Moulin Rouge would have Sammy Davis, Jr., on stage, with George Burns and Gracie Allen, Nat "King" Cole, Jack Benny and Mary Livingston, Joe E. Lewis, Frank Sinatra, Peter Lawford, and Harry Belafonte, and 350 others watching the hottest show in Las Vegas from the audience.

While all these people were watching the Watusi being danced by the Moulin Rouge chorus line of 23 gorgeous girls, the dealers in pit three at the Desert Inn were talking to one another. The place was empty. And the Flamingo began letting craps dealers go home early.

The night the Dunes opened, May 23, 1955, Frank Sinatra was in the house. He played, he saw the show, and then at 10:30 he escorted Hedda Hopper over to the Moulin Rouge to watch the Tropi-Can-Can and the Watusi. The Dunes people were not happy. On their opening night, Sinatra and party left early to head out to West Las Vegas.

And when Sinatra showed up somewhere, everyone else wanted to be there, too.

"Holy Mackerel - Did You See Our Crowd Last Night?"

"I saw Marlene Dietrich with Sinatra! And George Burns was there again! Damn!"

And sure enough, the gamblers wanted to be where the action was. So instead of staying at the Flamingo to gamble, even the tourists wanted to try out the Rouge where they heard the action really was.

Surprisingly, few newspaper or magazine articles were written about what happened. Good records were not kept, apparently. And there weren't many people who wrote about the history of the place.

In the second floor executive offices at the Sands and the Flamingo and the DI, people started to take the Moulin Rouge seriously. At first, it seemed like a nice, innocent enterprise for Negroes, which didn't have a snowball's chance in hell of succeeding. It was in West Las Vegas, after all. "Who is going to drive to West Vegas to play 21 next to a bunch of Negroes?" was the common thought.

But night after night the midnight show at the Moulin Rouge and the breakfast show were selling out. And then the dinner show began taking off, and the gaming tables were beginning to fill up every night. The casino owners assumed that the Moulin Rouge was going to attract blacks only, but, to nearly everyone's surprise, the casino was filled with white gamblers. Dressed to the T's – diamonds, black chips, loud voices, celebrities walking around, hundred dollar bills filling up the drop boxes at the tables. It was heady stuff.

Finally, enough was enough.

The showgirls who were going over to the Moulin Rouge for the breakfast show were told by their managers that if they were seen there again, they would be fired.

The liquor distributor who was supplying one of the Strip hotels was told that if he kept selling to the Moulin Rouge, he could forget their business.

The food purveyor to another hotel was asked who he wanted to keep as a client, the hotel or the Moulin Rouge?

Then, the liquor license of the Moulin Rouge was suspended.

Next to the gaming license, a casino's liquor license is the most valuable commodity it has.

In researching why the liquor license of the Moulin Rouge was lifted, I found only one paragraph in one of the Las Vegas newspapers. The Moulin Rouge was accused of charging "working blacks" more money for drinks than they were charging "white-collar blacks," and, therefore, were practicing discrimination.

One sunny afternoon in October, federal agents and agents from the state of Nevada Gaming Commission and the Clark County Sheriff's Office entered the casino portion of the Moulin Rouge, told everyone to stop what they were doing, and literally closed the casino.

Newspaper reports said many of the gamblers grabbed as many hundred-dollar chips as they could and headed for the front doors. Other players gathered their chips and got on line at the one casino cage hoping to cash in their chips. They were told by Sheriff's Deputies that the cashier was closed and they would have to file in Clark County Court for redemption of their chips, which were now under control of the Nevada Gaming Commission.

And that was that.

There wasn't much coverage of the closing. The hotel, which opened to such fanfare, covered by the national news, upon closing barely received passing references in the Las Vegas newspapers. Only a few brief articles appeared about the closing in all the print media throughout the fall of 1955. Curious.

It wasn't as if the *Las Vegas Sun* or Hank Greenspun's *Review Journal* were shy. Over the years, they took on the Mafia in Vegas, they went after the casino owners, even the governor of the state was called a crook. Why didn't they make a big deal out of the sudden closing of the Moulin Rouge?

The few articles on the topic suggest three possible reasons for its closing – poor location, poor management, and a glut of new hotel rooms. Baloney!

The place was coming apart at the seams with business. The Cafe Rouge was the only showroom in Las Vegas that was continuously selling out. And that includes the Copa Room at the Sands, the Arabian Room at the Dunes, and the Venus Showroom at the New Frontier.

One might try to blame the country's economic downswing. Several hotels were having trouble at the time. The Dunes, for example, was right on the brink of bankruptcy when it closed for remodeling before it was bailed out by Jakie Freedman of the Sands. The Riviera, which had just opened, was losing enormous amounts of money. The Royal Nevada closed altogether.

But the Moulin Rouge was making money. The place was jumping. For its small size, it was turning into a gold mine!

Then suddenly, the big five began to apply pressure on the two Las Vegas banks to call in the short-term notes that had been made to the Moulin Rouge investors. And they applied pressure on the suppliers of the Moulin Rouge, demanding money out front for liquor deliveries or food on a daily basis.

It was rumored that the owners of the Moulin Rouge were stealing the hotel blind. One of the night auditors was quoted by a *Las Vegas Sun* reporter, "Money was flying out the back door!" A perfectly plausible explanation. The owners were stealing money from the soft count room at the MR. Not the first time it had happened, and certainly not the last time either.

But then, one asks, "What is the Nevada Gaming Commission ... stupid?" They licensed eight guys to operate a gambling establishment in Nevada. They also sent in one of their NGC people daily to watch what was going on. The state of Nevada and the federal government made every effort to make sure gambling revenues weren't being pocketed by owners. And they know what forensic accounting is. When they closed the Moulin Rouge, they took the books.

If there was money missing, do you think the two or three government agencies who were going over the Rouge's books would miss it? Nor report it? If they found someone's hand in the till, do you think they'd just shrug their shoulders and leave?

Same year – 1955, Al Parvin was convicted of stealing $30 million from the Flamingo, and he went to jail. Morris Lansburg was convicted of stealing from the Flamingo and the Fremont. And when James Tanner, Maury Freeman, and William Pompili were caught stealing from the Frontier, they went to jail.

Then there was Morris Kleinman at the Riv. He was caught embezzling money from the Riviera and was sent to federal prison for three years. When Gus Greenbaum was caught stealing from the Riviera, his head was cut off, literally.

So, if the hotel was doing well, and there was nothing amiss with the books, I've always wondered why the MR closed like that. Just one of those Las Vegas mysteries of history.

There has always been talk that the MR was forced out of business by the owners of the five big Strip hotels and Benny Binion of the Horseshoe. And then there's the fact that one of the executives from the Moulin Rouge was given a really nice job at the Desert Inn right after the closing, but it's just talk.

After the casino closed, the Moulin Rouge operated as a hotel for a few years.

In 1960 it was used for a historic signing of an agreement to abolish housing and other forms of racial segregation on the Strip.

In May 2003, an arsonist's fire destroyed what remained of the Moulin Rouge.

VEGAS SHOWGIRLS

1957 July - *Minsky's Goes to Paris* at the Dunes is generally thought to be the first of the nude shows in Las Vegas. Bill Miller produced the entire show for $9,000.

1958 July – *Lido de Paris* opened at the Stardust. The Lido would run for 31 years, which was a longer run than the original *Lido* in Paris.

1958 August – *Folies Bergere* opened at the Tropicana.

Beautiful Lisa Malouf Medford, shown here in a 1961 photo at the Tropicana, was the first nude showgirl in Las Vegas.

In 1961, when Lisa Medford was on the stage of the Tropicana, the showroom manager was a man named Joe Agosto. Joe was later convicted of actually running the money end of the Trop, the casino. Joe Agosto was Mr. Inside for the Civella Family of Kansas City. Lisa was on stage, and Agosto and another Tropicana executive named Carl Thomas were in the counting room making sure that Kansas City was kept happy.

Four months before Minsky's, in February of 1957, Lisa opened with Harry Belafonte at the Riviera. And the Riviera decided to be the first to try out the new Las Vegas city ordinance allowing nudity, with the provision that the nude showgirl was not allowed to move the entire time she was on stage. Lisa was a "standing nude."

FRANK COSTELLO BUILDS
THE TROPICANA

Located at the southernmost end of the Strip, the Tropicana opened in April 1957 with 300 rooms and at a final cost of nearly $15 million. When the Tropicana was being presented to investors, the prospectus stated, "Total cost to open ... $4 million!"

This photo was taken on May 4, 1957. A full month after the Tropicana opened, the casino still wasn't open. The Gaming Commission wouldn't license any of the principals until Louis Lederer and Colonel Chas (Babe) Baron came along. They were licensed, and the Tropicana casino opened.

The 1950s was the boom decade for Las Vegas, especially for the construction trades.

With five major casinos being built at the same time, union laborers were commanding double wages as their straight time. One of the reasons that the hotels ran into such cost overruns was that the skilled labor market was drying up fast. A union journeyman plumber or electrician or mason or carpenter could get wealthy working in Las Vegas in the 1950s.

One of the expressions used around Las Vegas was an "Outside Man." It's the opposite of the "Inside Man."

If two guys go into partnership in a shoe manufacturing business, one of the guys knows the plant and who to order the laces from, and how to make sure the utility bills are paid on time, things like that ... that's the Inside Man.

Now, supposing the company who you and your partner have been ordering laces from for all these years becomes the only lace company in your town. They bought out their competition, and now, instead of selling you the laces you need for 19 cents each, the price, as of next Monday, will be 45 cents each.

The Inside Man calls and complains and makes noises and tells the laces guys that this price increase is going to force him out of business, and, *"We did business with your father, rest his soul, and I'm your oldest customer, and if it wasn't for me and my partner, you'd still be selling string on the street instead of laces in your fancy factory, you thief bastard!"*

Of course you know you're going to have to pay the 45 cents. You already yelled at the supplier, you called him a name, and he still wasn't going to go back on his back-breaking prices.

Now the definition of "Outside Man."

Your partner is supposed to take care of problems like this when they occur. You call your partner at home and explain the situation to him. *"Oh my, I hope he can make our laces manufacturer shave a few cents off his price – we just can't pay 45 cents for laces and still make a profit."* Outside Man (OM) knows that they not only have to make a profit, they also have to pocket a little each week to keep their wives,

Mrs. OM and Mrs. IM, happy. They think of it as their "skimming operation." And cooking the books to make it look legit was one of the things the IM does well.

So IM timorously picks up the phone and calls his partner, though it's close to 10 p.m. already. OM says, *"Hey buddy, don't worry about it! That's what I'm here for. I wouldn't come into the plant and decide what kind of leather we should buy for the wingtips you want to make next year. That's your area, you're the IM, buddy, and you do it great!"*

"Please don't give it another thought, don't lose any sleep over this at all. I'll explain to him our situation, and the inherent unfairness of his trying to exploit a situation like this. He's been a reasonable man for many years, I'm sure if I explain things to him, maybe using a pie-chart, he'll see reason."

"Thanks, OM, I really can go to sleep now."

That evening at 3:40 a.m., Outside Man arrives at the laces supplier's home. He rings the doorbell once (shhh...don't want to wake the neighbors) and then a second time. Finally a downstairs light comes on, and his laces supplier answers the door in his robe and tousled hair. The OM blows his fucking head off with both barrels of a 12-gauge short barrel shotgun. And then goes home.

In the morning, the surviving partner in the lace factory calls Mr. OM and asks how much he'd like to pay for the laces. They agree on 4 cents. *"But I'm going to pay it to you over time. You got a problem with that, surviving partner?"*

Whether you recognize it or not, this method of contract negotiations is now taught in nearly every MBA program in the country.

The Inside Man also was responsible for making sure the skim worked well, and that the Mob's money, every cent of it, got to the Mob. The Inside Man could always be found in the counting room making sure that the Mob got its cut before the money was reported, deposited, and taxed.

The problem was that all the Mobs were trying to keep Las Vegas as tourist-friendly as possible. That meant the activities of the Mobs had to be unobservable to the common visitor. Now with seven or eight major Mobs present in Las Vegas, and each watching out for its own interests, there were lots of Outside Men on the Strip.

With so many different crime families represented in Las Vegas, and so much money in the counting rooms, there was a lot of temptation in a concentrated area. Some Mob families began to build up a small army of soldiers in Las Vegas. And everyone knew where that was going to lead.

The best Outside Men were ruthless, and in some cases psychotic. Soon, there would be too many murderers in Las Vegas. Something huge was bound to happen. And when it happened, it was going to affect every one of the Mobs.

Tony Accardo, boss of Chicago, called for a meeting of all the Mob leaders around the country who were making a nice living off the skim from their Vegas casinos.

In the late 1950s, the skim taken from the various Las Vegas casinos was about $1 million a day! That figure is accepted by most of the Las Vegas and Mob historians, and it's the figure that's mentioned in the FBI reports.

At the sit-down of the Mob bosses, Accardo explained, "Together all we're accomplishing is scarin' the fuck'n tourists back to Iowa." He suggested that there be only one Outside Man in Las Vegas who could take care of everyone's interests.

According to William F. Roemer, Jr., in his book, *War of the Godfathers*, the families reached an "accommodation." Las Vegas was going to be under the eye of the Chicago Outfit. They were in first and the city was theirs. Las Vegas would be a wide open city, any Mob could do business there, but Chicago was responsible for protecting all their interests.

Chicago would supply the Outside Man for all the Mobs. One man who any Inside Man could go to regardless of what group he represented. If there was a problem, Chicago's Outside Man would get it solved.

Tony Accardo and Sam Giancana, Tony's Las Vegas specialist, sat down to discuss who they would send to Las Vegas.

Accardo was thinking that he'd keep Johnny Roselli in place. Roselli was doing a good job representing Chicago in both Las Vegas and Hollywood.

Roselli was currently living at the Desert Inn working as the Mob's West Coast Outside Man. At the same time, Roselli made sure that the movie studios' interests in Hollywood and the Chicago Outfit's interests were one and the same. Accardo decided enough was at stake to make Roselli Outside Man in Las Vegas full-time.

Sam Giancana agreed that Johnny Roselli was doing an adequate job in Las Vegas, but he was spread too thin. Because of his excellent Hollywood connections, Giancana said, Johnny should be sent to Hollywood full-time. Sam thought Marshall Caifano would do a better job in Vegas.

Finally, Caifano was chosen. He had all the requisites needed for the job.

While working for the Mob in Chicago, Caifano was responsible for a string of really gruesome killings, many involving a blowtorch.

He was a prime suspect in the brutal killing of 18-year-old Estelle Carey, a chip girl at one of the Chicago Outfit's illegal clubs. She probably pocketed some chips, and she ended up with her face burned off. Caifano loved that blowtorch!

There were a few reasons why Giancana wanted Marshall to go to Vegas. First, he knew that he was sending out a ruthless killer who would keep everyone in line. There was real fear when Marshall Caifano walked into a room.

Then there was Darlene. Marshall Caifano's wife. Giancana had a thing for Darlene Caifano. Darlene had a thing for Sam Giancana, too. When Marshall was out attending to Mob business, much of it out of the city, Darlene and Sam would get together.

One of the first times Caifano went to Las Vegas, he had his name changed legally to John Marshall. He was one of the scariest people ever in Las Vegas. However, in his job description, being a scary person was near the top job qualification. Caifano was there to be Mr. Outside Man for the Mobs.

Soon, Caifano was feared by everyone in Vegas. Word on the street was that all the big Las Vegas hits were on his resume. Finally, in 1960, after the fire that burned the El Rancho Vegas to the ground, the Chicago Outfit was ready to make the change. The Mob was convinced that Caifano was no longer the public "face" that the Chicago Outfit wanted in Las Vegas. They replaced Caifano with Johnny Roselli.

Johnny Roselli. A favorite of mine, Roselli became not only Chicago's point-man in Las Vegas, but the go-between for most of the Mob factions and the hotels and casinos on the Strip. Comfortable and accepted by friends in the Mobs and among hotel owners alike, Johnny Roselli was as tough as Marshall Caifano was, but much smoother.

Roselli's very first job in Las Vegas was putting together a working partnership for the Tropicana. It was a neatly woven combination of the most powerful Mobsters in the country, all partners in the new $50-million Las Vegas hotel/casino.

The Tropicana partners included Roselli's bosses in Chicago: Sam Giancana; Paul "the Waiter" Ricca; Camel Humphries; and Meyer Lansky, who was commuting between

Havana, Cuba, and his home in Miami; Frank Costello, representing the New York Families; and Carlos Marcello of New Orleans.

What was unusual was that all these Mobs from different cities were partnering in the same hotel venture.

Fronting for the Chicago Outfit was Ben Jaffe. He owned the giant Fountainbleu Hotel in Miami, and also owned an insurance company in Indiana. Ben's local Las Vegas partner was Las Vegas native, JK Houssels, Sr., "Kell" to his friends.

Dandy Phil Kastel worked for Arnold Rothstein. Had Rothstein been born 30 years later, he would have loved Las Vegas.

He was the inspiration for Meyer Wolfsheim in *The Great Gatsby*, and Nathan Detroit in *Guys and Dolls*. He was rumored to be the mastermind of the "Black Sox" scandal and the fixing of the 1919 World Series.

Called Mr. Broadway, he had his own booth at Lindy's Restaurant in Manhattan. Dandy Phil rubbed elbows with the celebrities that always seemed to hang around Rothstein. People like Nicky Arnstein and Fanny Brice and Gertrude Vanderbilt. Arnold Rothstein was also a gambler.

Dandy was very happy in the Rothstein gang. He made lots of money with rum running and extortion, big-time gambling, some loan sharking, a little bootlegging – all growth industries. And a fellow like Dandy Phil, who was pretty damn ruthless and very bright, did very well as Arnold Rothstein's lieutenant.

Then, the day before the 1928 Presidential elections, Arnold Rothstein, who was one of the "whales" in New York poker games, was playing in one of the famous "Broadway Games" a 48-hour poker marathon. At the end of the 48 hours, Rothstein had lost $320,000. He felt he was cheated by two guys who were probably playing partners in the game, and he refused to pay.

Two weeks after the game, he was murdered in his apartment at the Park Central Hotel in New York. Nate "Nig" Raymond and "Titanic" Thomas were the two men who beat him in the game, and they were the prime suspects in the murder. However, no charges were ever filed, and the 1928 murder is still unsolved

There were some New Yorkers who were very happy that Arnold Rothstein was no more – among them Dutch Schultz, Louis Lepke, Joe "The Boss" Masseria, Frank Costello, and Meyer Lansky.

OK, Rothstein is history, and his first lieutenant is out of work. But Dandy Phil Kastel knew gambling very well. Frank Costello interviewed him and gave him a job.

In 1935, Frank Costello made a deal with then-Governor of Louisiana, Huey P. Long, for gambling rights in the state. Costello took over all gambling in Louisiana. He called his friend and Mob boss of New Orleans, Carlos Marcello, and told Carlos that he was sending Dandy Phil down to work with Huey Long and make sure the state of Louisiana gets a fair shake, and to "make damn sure we get our cut every single week."

By the early 1950s, Dandy Phil was still doing a wonderful job. Louisiana gambling was running smooth as silk, and Frank Costello was paying more and more attention to Las Vegas. There was some very big cash money being made out there. Frank called Dandy and told him to think about moving to Las Vegas. "I'll find you something there. Don't worry, Dandy. Haven't we always done well together before?"

Frank Costello wanted to build a hotel and casino in Las Vegas. He needed only two things to make it happen: someone to put up the money and someone to run it for him. He also knew that there was no way the Nevada Tax Commission was going to approve anything that he was involved in.

"I want you to go over to Miami and meet with Ben Jaffe over at the Fountainbleu," Frank continued. "Got it?" (Word on the street was that Frank Costello owned the giant hotel, and Ben Jaffe was fronting for him.) Dandy Phil and Ben Jaffe sat down and began planning the Tropicana Hotel in Las Vegas.

Costello wanted to own the lion's share of the Tropicana, but two groups were formed to put up the money for the new enterprise:

The Kastel group consisted of Dandy Phil Kastel, Frank Costello, Carlos Marcello, and the singer Morton Downey. Among the four of them, they had $1 million in cash. But they needed $3 million more to build the hotel.

Ben Jaffe and his partner, Charles "Babe" Baron, and his friend, Phil Galp, had $3 million. Galp owned Taylor Construction Company of Miami, which had built the Riviera a year earlier, and he loved Las Vegas.

A deal was struck. Conquistador, Inc., was formed with Morton Downey, Frank Costello, Carlos Marcello, and Dandy Phil Kastel as partners. They put up their million, and Ben Jaffe put up $3 million in cash and the Fountainbleu Hotel as collateral for an additional line of credit, "just in case it's needed." The Tropicana Hotel was ready to come off the drawing boards.

Ben Jaffe and Dandy Phil Kastel flew out to Las Vegas, Ben purchased 40 acres of land, and construction of the Tropicana Hotel began.

Soon, cost overruns and skimming of construction funds forced Jaffe to sell his Fountainbleu Hotel in Miami for $3 million. The money was needed desperately, and he was already on the hook for $3 mil.

And then there was Margaret Kastel. As much as Dandy Phil loved the idea of being in charge of a big Las Vegas Casino, his wife, Margaret, loved the idea even more. She wanted to and expected to decorate the place!

Margaret Kastel – Mrs. Tropicana. There are many wonderful stories about this woman and the building of the Tropicana. There are many people who believe that Margaret Kastel single-handedly caused over $1 million in cost overruns.

She'd show up at the worksite every day in her three-quarter-length mink coat; and with a 10-inch cigarette holder waving and pointing, she'd "advise" the workmen on what they should be doing and accuse them of not working very hard. She certainly did not care about construction basics; "What do you mean, it's a load bearing wall? It's ugly. I want glass and mirrors!"

When more money was needed, Ben borrowed another $3 million from the insurance company he owned in Indiana to pour into "His Tropicana." This time, the $3 million loan hurt his insurance company – and it also raised a little red flag in a few regulatory agencies.

Also during this time, the world's largest hotel, the Stardust, was being built. Tony Cornero, who was building it, was driven to get the project finished, so he started paying skilled construction people twice union wages to work on the Stardust. That started a bidding war for construction crews and material.

But despite all the road blocks, by April Fool's Day, 1957, the ribbon-cutting ceremony was held, champagne was flowing all through the Executive Suite, and the owners of record and the owners off the record were all congratulating themselves. They were ready to start making some money!

Two of the more stylish men in Las Vegas were Dandy Phil Kastel who wore silk suits and handmade shirts and walked with a gold-tipped walking stick; and Johnny Roselli, who had a penchant for $300 slacks, wore a three-carat diamond pinkie ring, and enjoyed seeing his barber twice a week.

But no one made fun of Johnny Roselli. Behind the smile was the Chicago Outfit's #1 enforcer in Las Vegas. He probably was personally responsible for 25 murders, but none in Las Vegas, of course! Anyway, Dandy Phil and Johnny Roselli got along very well. Dandy Phil was responsible for the hotel portion of the Tropicana, and Johnny Roselli took over the responsibility of the casino.

Roselli brought in the following:

Lou Lederer, with whom he had worked in Chicago, to run the casino

Babe Baron to be the casino host and attract high rollers

Harry Drucker, the world-renowned Beverly Hills barber, to set up a barber shop in the Trop

Alex Perino, owner of Perino's restaurant of Beverly Hills, to become executive chef

Mike Tanico, husband of Dandy Phil's niece, as head cashier at the Trop

As a "perk" for putting the deal together, Johnny Roselli was given the concessions, always a wonderful moneymaker at a Strip resort.

Roselli had the hotel gift shop, the parking concession, and he was in charge of booking all entertainment for both the main showroom and the Showcase Lounge. And he was paying himself 15 percent of all fees, which meant his first year's income from the Tropicana was going to be over a $1 million. That was a lot of money in 1957.

Then the Nevada Gaming Commission threw a wrench in the activities. Because Dandy Phil and Frank Costello were known associates, the Commission refused to let Dandy have a gambling license.

At the last minute, the casino operations were turned over to Kell Houssels, leaving Lou Lederer in place running the counting rooms and cashiers' cages, and Babe Baron remaining as credit manager. April 4, 1957, the Tropicana, with 300 rooms, finally opened.

The initial figure of $4 million had become $15 million.

From the very first day the Tropicana opened, it lost money. It just wasn't bringing in the bigger gamblers, skimming was everywhere, and it seemed as if the gamblers who did play the Tropicana were running very lucky.

No one was more upset than Frank Costello with the way things were going at the Trop. But he had bigger problems, at home, in New York, with another Mob family – the Genoveses.

In New York, Frank Costello lived in the elegant Majestic Hotel on Park Avenue West. On the morning of May 2, 1957, he was leaving his apartment building when a lone gunman walked up to him and shot him once in the head with a .38 police special. The gunman was an up-and-coming button man for Mafia boss Vito Genovese.

It should have been a successful hit. Costello was the most powerful member of the Mafia in the US, and usually traveled with one or even two bodyguards, but apparently this morning, his bodyguard had called in sick.

The gunman, probably Chin Gigante, walked up to Costello as Frank was leaving his apartment house, and nervously said, "This is for you, Frank," and shot once at point blank range. The gunman bolted into a waiting Cadillac. But he left too soon. The wound was only superficial.

Costello was brought unconscious to Roosevelt Hospital, just a few blocks away, and while doctors were working on him, the New York Police went through his clothing. In the inside pocket of his blood stained suit jacket was a note which said:

> Gross casino wins as of 4/27/57 $651,284
>
> Casino wins less markers 434,695
>
> Slot wins 62,844
>
> Markers 153,745
>
> Mike $150 a week, totaling $600
>
> Jake $100 a week, totaling $400
>
> L. - $30,000; H. - $9,000

The doctors released Costello later that night. The botched assassination had only grazed his skull behind his right ear, and he was brought to the West 54th Street Police Station for questioning.

"I don't know nothin'," was all Costello would say. Within a month, he was called before a Senate Subcommittee on Organized Crime. It was one of many Senate visits that Frank Costello was to make during the 1950s. When asked about the note found in his pocket, he took the Fifth Amendment – 22 times.

The New York Police and the New York District Attorney's office found the Las Vegas connection to the note within two days. The details in the note matched exactly to the posted receipts at the Trop on April 27.

Another interesting detail about the note – it was signed with the initials of three people:

LJL - Louis J. Lederer who was in charge of all gaming at the Trop

JKH - JK (Kell) Houssels who was casino manager for the Trop

ROC - Robert O'Cannon who was the general manager of the hotel and on duty that night

Agents from the Nevada Gaming Control Board (NGCB) and the Las Vegas Sheriff's Department came into the Tropicana casino and told Louis Lederer, casino boss, to leave the casino floor. He was forced by the Nevada Gaming Commission to resign from the hotel and sell his 7 percent ownership in the Tropicana.

Frank Costello was the hidden owner of the Tropicana. This photo was taken in 1956 just before he began a one-year prison sentence for income tax evasion.

As this was happening, new men came into the Tropicana. Lou Walters, Barbara Walters' father, was the producer of a new show that was going to run for many years at the Tropicana, the fabulous Folies Bergere.

And there was a guy in the background of the showroom where the Follies were playing. His business card said, Joe Agosto, Tropicana Hotel Showroom Manager. He was sent to Las Vegas from Kansas City along with Carl Thomas of the Civella Mob in KC.

And for the next few years, unassuming Joe Agosto would operate one of the more elegant skimming operations on the Strip while the Tropicana's casino supported the Civella crime family in Kansas City with millions of dollars a year.

Concidentally, Ben Jaffe, who decided he better try to salvage whatever he could in Miami, was still waiting for a cab to take him to McCarran Airport when Dandy and Margaret Kastel drove away, and Joe Agosto and Carl Thomas walked in the front door of the Tropicana.

DOES THE RIVIERA STILL KILL ITS EXECUTIVES?

Three brothers, David, Meyer, and Lou Gensburg, owned one of the world's largest pinball machine companies. Like so many others who loved Las Vegas, their dream was to own their own casino. And they had the money to live out that dream. To actually own their own casino. To actually own their own hotel. To actually own their own counting room with all that money. It nearly brings tears to your eyes.

And thanks to that wonderful Senator Estes Kefauver and his Organized Crime Committee Hearings, which were on TV every single afternoon in 1951, and thanks to the United States Senate, the Gensburg brothers found Tony Accardo.

The Kefauver Committee asked Accardo about Las Vegas and hidden ownership of some of the hotels, and how money was being skimmed out of their casinos. Obviously Tony Accardo was an expert, so he was the guy that the three Gensburg brothers wanted to speak with.

In 1952, Tony Accardo was with the Outfit, the Chicago Mob. Paul Ricca was Mob boss, Tony Accardo was the number two man – and handled the day-by-day everything that had to do with the Outfit.

The Gensburgs got his phone number and asked him if they could take him out for lunch. "It involves money, Mr. Accardo." The Gensburgs were well known in Chicago. They were very wealthy men, and Tony knew who they were.

Accardo and the Gensburg brothers sat down together. The situation was laid out fairly quickly, and all the men in the room knew that this was going to be a profitable arrangement for everyone. A very upbeat meeting.

The Gensburg brothers wanted to own a big casino in Las Vegas. Accardo told the Gensburgs that their business venture had his blessings. He wished them the best of luck, and after they opened their casino out in Las Vegas, he'd come out and give them all kinds of action.

Tony or "Joe Batters," a nickname Al Capone had given him: *"Easiest way to solve an argument is with a bat, right?"* Tony had three very talented men on his payroll that he wanted the Gensburgs to get together with: the Fischetti brothers, Rocco, Charles, and Joe. Accardo set up a meeting and told them that Joe Fischetti was the expert in casino acquisition. The Gensburgs shook hands with the Fischetti brothers, and so began the Casa Blanca Hotel project in Las Vegas. By cutting the Chicago Outfit in on their new venture, the Gensburgs decided that they were almost guaranteeing its success.

David, Meyer, and Lou Gensburg went to Las Vegas. After two days of driving around, they found a perfect lot, exactly where the Casa Blanca Hotel and Casino should be.

The very next day, through the bank in Las Vegas, they purchased the property for cash. A cashier's check. Just north of the Thunderbird. On the other side of the lot they bought, Milton Prell was just developing another big resort hotel to be called the Sahara.

And they found the right architect, and Taylor Construction of Miami, owned by Phil Galp. Galp and family moved to Las Vegas; building the Casa Blanca would be a 24-hour-a-day, seven-day-a-week commitment.

Joe Fischetti was of assistance to them here. With the help of Harry Silbert, the Gensburgs' Beverly Hills attorney, the brothers would soon own the Casa Blanca. And they were going to lease the hotel to themselves. They were going to collect $500,000 per year rent on the place, as all casino rentals are paid in advance. During the 1950s and 1960s most of the Strip hotels were on leaseback arrangements – a standard finance arrangement.

Next Step: Get the license from the Nevada Tax Commission

The Fischettis wanted to get two of their people on the license for the hotel, Charles Tourine, (aka Charles White), who was willing to invest $200,000 for 4 percent interest in the Casa Blanca, and William Bishoff (aka Lefty Clark).

Bishoff belonged to the Detroit Syndicate and had been a casino operator in Havana for Meyer Lansky. Charles Tourine, affectionately known as Charley "the Blade," had also been working in Havana as casino manager of the beautiful Capri casino.

Just before the Tax Commission was about to meet, realizing that he really didn't have a snowball's chance of being approved, Charles Tourine withdrew his offer for $200,000 and asked that his name be removed from the license application.

Obviously, this raised suspicions, and it slowed down the licensing processing. Bishoff was turned down by the Commission also. A couple of other original investors removed their names from the gaming license application, and the now-cleaned application was submitted to the Nevada Tax Commission.

On Sept. 22, 1953, the final group of applicants signed their forms and applied to the NTC for licensing. Approved was the Riviera Hotel (the name was changed from the Casa Blanca to the Riviera just before this meeting). The list of owners, approved by the Nevada Tax Commission and percentage of ownership:

David Gensburg (15%), president of the hotel

Meyer Gensburg (15%), work full-time at the hotel

Lou Gensberg (12%), work full-time at the hotel

R. H. Bailey (10%), New York contractor

Jack Goldman (15%), Miami and NYC restaurants

Murray Saul (10%), Miami land developer

Harry Robbins (15%), Beverly Hills attorney

Harpo (Arthur) Marx (5%), movie star, comedian

Gummo (Milton) Marx (3%), comedian

Thus the construction of the Riviera – the ninth Las Vegas Strip hotel – was started. The groundbreaking ceremony was held May 27, 1954.

While the giant Riviera, the first of the high-rise resorts on the Las Vegas Strip, was being built, just a mile or so south, Gus Greenbaum and his wife, Bess, were talking about finally selling the Flamingo and retiring to Phoenix.

For the last eight years, Gus Greenbaum had run the Flamingo. Greenbaum was the second owner of the Flamingo.

The Reign of Ben Siegel had lasted only six months at the Flamingo; the Reign of Gus Greenbaum had lasted eight years.

Eight years of playing too hard and drinking too hard had taken their toll on Gus, and over the objections of his partners, Gus spoke with "Big Tuna" (Tony Accardo), his boss in Chicago, about leaving Vegas and retiring in Phoenix. Accardo said fine, that Gus had given enough years and his health to the Flamingo, and if he and his wife wanted to go home to Phoenix, it was OK with him.

Happily, Gus emptied his office at the Flamingo, packed up his white Cadillac with the trailer behind it, packed up some egg salad sandwiches for the road, and he and Bess drove home to Phoenix, looking forward to their retirement, singing a good part of the way.

The beautiful Ruth Gillis. Ruth was one of the original Riviera showgirls, opening with Liberace on April 20, 1955. She remained in show business for many years and knew many of the characters in this book.

This was in March of 1955. Tony Accardo and the Chicago Outfit already had new owners lined up to take over the Flamingo. A large group of investors headed up by Tom Hull (the guy who had built the El Rancho Vegas a dozen years earlier) was now going to be the owner of record of the Fabulous Flamingo.

It wasn't a bad deal for the new owners. The final selling price was just at $7 million, and the owners (a total of 32 of them) had to come up with only $975,000 down. Chicago would finance the remaining $6.25 million – what's generally called a "sweetheart deal!"

So far, this was lining up as a win-win situation – at least on paper.

Gus and Bess could play golf in the afternoons, Tom Hull and his group had their hands on a profitable hotel. When Gus left the Flamingo, it was showing millions of dollars a year in reported profits, plus a few bucks extra for owners back in Chicago. Smart Tony Accardo had just guaranteed himself millions of new dollars a year from the new owners. Just another wonderful Las Vegas story!

A month after Gus retired, April 1955, the new Riviera was ready to open. Nine stories high – $10 million to build – the first high-rise on the Strip.

The Riv lost money its first day of operation, and continued losing money every day for the next three months. Well beyond the honeymoon period.

The Gensburg brothers and their partners were all bright men, but none had any experience in casino operations, and it showed. These guys were used to operating the big tourist hotels along Collins Avenue in Miami. And running a hotel and running a giant casino require different talents.

In 1955 there was a practice among casino owners called "Filling the Journal."

In 1954, the *Las Vegas Review Journal* began distribution in Las Vegas. It started modestly as a 12-page paper, one that could be easily folded and put under your arm comfortably.

The soft count room was where most of the early casino owners preferred to be, more than anywhere else in the world. The money in there was their money – they won it fair and square! They covered a bet a customer made, and they won the bet. This money was theirs!

Gorgeous Kim Krantz was one of the most beautiful showgirls at the Riviera in 1955.

So, if an owner walked into the soft count room with his thin little *Las Vegas Review Journal* folded under his arm, and he came out with a BIG FAT *Las Vegas Review Journal* folded under his arm, who was going to stop him? It's conjecture, of course, but word on the street has always been that there were way too many people in the Riviera front office who were "filling their journals" – but that's just word on the street.

There's no question that the opening of the Riv was bad timing. No one's fault. It was 1955, and there was a general recession in the country; less excess income meant fewer visitors.

Plus, there were lots and lots of new hotels opening about the same time as the Riviera. The Dunes was weeks away from opening; the Sahara had expanded with a new wing; the Showboat and the New Frontier had opened; and the Hacienda was just being finished. All of these hotels were on the Strip. Though not an obvious threat yet, the Moulin Rouge had just opened in West Las Vegas. It would turn out to draw away thousands from the Strip.

Add to that the fact that the Gensburgs and their partners believed that they had found Nirvana in the soft count room. It's very possible that they began helping themselves to way too much money from the beginning, and it was beginning to become obvious.

A casino ain't supposed to lose money day after day after day, week after week after week. Eventually the laws of probability have to take over.

Now, Tony Accardo had absolutely no sense of humor at all. The Riviera, which was supposed to make lots of money for the Mob, was costing everyone involved in the hotel both money and blood pressure! Week after week, more and more money was being poured into the Riviera, and week after week it was going further into debt.

Tony Accardo called and caught Gus Greenbaum just before he was leaving home.

Accardo told him that he'd be out in Phoenix this Thursday at 9 a.m., and "me and everyone in the Outfit wants you to consider coming out of this damn retirement, and taking over the Riviera. Vegas is where you belong, Gus."

Tony Accardo and Jake Guzik flew to Phoenix. "Gus, we really want you to run the Riviera for us." But Gus really didn't want to go back.

In a series of three meetings at the Flame Night Club, Accardo insisted that he "wouldn't take 'no' for an answer" and laid out his plans.

Jake Guzik reminded Gus that he still owed Accardo over a million dollars from a loan which Gus had accepted when he was at the Flamingo.

Tony knew that with Greenbaum in charge of the Riviera, it would turn into a cash-cow, and quickly too. Gus Greenbaum was feared by all his employees. It's how he got things done. Everyone who worked for him was afraid of him. He wouldn't hesitate for a second crushing a dealer's hands in a vice, or using a baseball bat on one of the cashiers who thought he could get that $100 bill into his pocket.

By the third meeting at the Flame Night Club, Tony Accardo was getting tired of listening to Gus' reasons why he couldn't take over the ownership of the Riv.

He was a sick man, Gus protested, the frenetic tempo in Las Vegas would kill him. Accardo, boss of the Chicago Outfit, pointed out that a man could die in a number of ways.

Gus could not be persuaded. He wasn't going back to Las Vegas. Period!

Four or five nights later, Gus got a phone call at 3 a.m. from his brother, Charlie Greenbaum. Charlie and his wife, Lenore, had to come over right now!

"But Charlie," said Gus, "it's 3 a.m. ... can't this wait until the morning?"

Lenore grabbed the phone from her husband, and in hysterics told Gus that she had just gotten a death threat. She was told by a voice on the phone that she had better talk to Gus, her brother-in-law, and persuade him to move back to Las Vegas, or else!

Gus assured her she had nothing to fear, it was a bluff. But the next morning Leone Greenbaum applied for a permit for a hand gun. Scottsdale PD also told her she had nothing to worry about; it was an empty threat.

Two nights later, Charlie Greenbaum came home and found his wife dead in their bed. The County Medical Examiner's inquest results said she "had been smothered by a human hand."

Gus and Bess Greenbaum repacked the Caddy, got a U-Haul hitched behind it, and returned to Las Vegas.

Within a very short period of time, Gus had put together his old group of guys from the Flamingo. Among them, he came up with the money necessary to buy the Riviera Hotel and Casino.

Gus Greenbaum bought 27 percent of the Casino. The others and their holdings were as follows:

Elias Atol (9%)

Frank Atol (4%)

Fred Atol (4%)

Joe Rosenburg (7%)

Icepick Willie Alderman (7%)

Davie Berman (7%)

Kewpie Rich (2%)

Sid Wyman, who also had points in the Sands (10%)

Jack McElry (4%) and

Ben Goffstein was given 2% by Gus and made VP of Operations

The remainder was held back, as was common practice, for future investors.

When Gus moved into the owner's suite at the Riv, the casino was in real trouble. It was on the brink of bankruptcy, all caused by the Miami group who had just been kicked out. Liquor had been disappearing from the storerooms, which found its way into the owners' suites, and personal items like cars were being paid for through the Riviera bank accounts. Plus, the Miami group of owners were gambling big every night at the Riviera's casino, losing thousands of dollars and then tearing up the markers!

Time to kick butt! Gus Greenbaum made Joe Rosenburg casino boss. Davie Berman was to supervise casino shifts, and Moey Sedway was in charge of keeping things in order. Moey was suddenly everywhere, barking orders, scowling ferociously, and getting things done.

Down the street at the Fabulous Flamingo there was some real bitterness with the Riviera and with Gus Greenbaum.

When selling out to Tom Hull and his group, Gus had promised "non-competition" with the Flamingo. He told the new owners of the Flamingo that he wouldn't operate within five miles of the Flamingo for five years.

And to add insult to injury, Gus Greenbaum and Ben Goffstein had accidentally taken with them the set of ledgers containing the names of the Flamingo's Gold Card holders the day they left the Flamingo. And those ledgers, for their own safety, had been buried in the desert near Pahrump.

Now that they were dug up and dusted off, all the Riviera secretaries were busily mailing out gold engraved invitations to all the names on this Very-VIP list!

Soon business was booming at the Riviera. Gus Greenbaum had done it again!

Gus soon went back to his old habits that nearly took his life at the Flamingo. He was drinking heavily, playing craps for big, big stakes, and chasing all the showgirls and secretaries and Keno girls and cocktail waitresses, as well as the prostitutes who openly operated out of the Riviera.

One of Gus' buddies at this time was a man named Willie Bioff who, charitably, was a stoolie, a convicted panderer, an extortionist, a fink, and a union tough-guy.

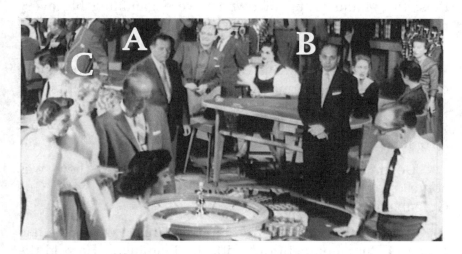

This photo was taken in early 1956, soon after the Miami group were sent packing and Gus Greenbaum became the new owner.

(A) **Ben Goffstein.** *Ben was a tough casino manager. He was Old School when it came to employees cheating the hotel. There were many busted hands and heads at the Riviera.*

(B) **Little Moey Sedway.** *Ben Siegel's assistant at the Flamingo; left during the clean sweep when Gus Greenbaum left.*

(C) *a gal named* **Lola** *who worked weekend nights at the Riviera. The fellow to her left, your right, is her uncle, "Uhh, sorry, what's your name again, honey?"*

Willie ran most of the important unions in Hollywood, and he made a lot of money extorting protection money from the major movie studios. Some years earlier, he had been tried and convicted of extorting money from Warner Brothers and Fox. They got him on violation of federal antiracketeering laws and sentenced him to 10 years in Leavenworth.

Three years into his sentence, Bioff and his partner, a fellow named George Brown, turned informers, and assisted the government in the prosecution of many of the Mafia people in Chicago. The exchange was having their own jail time reduced to "time served." Among the Mobsters Willie Bioff testified against were Frank Nitti (though Nitti committed suicide before his trial), Lou Campagna, Paul "the Waiter" Ricca, Johnny Roselli, Francis Maritone, and Lou Kaufman. A total of nine Chicago Mobsters were taken out of commission due to Willie Bioff. They were all convicted and given prison sentences, and Bioff was released from prison.

Bioff moved home to Phoenix as soon as he came out of prison, and, during his "retirement," he and Gus became friends. Chicago wasn't real happy with Gus Greenbaum befriending the fink, however. Besides Gus Greenbaum, Willie Bioff became friendly with the soon-to-be junior US Senator from Arizona, Barry Goldwater. Goldwater was very, very well known in Las Vegas. When Gus was at the Flamingo, Barry Goldwater and his brother Bobby Goldwater both held Gold Cards at the Flamingo, and now both the Goldwater brothers followed their friend Gus to the Riviera.

Because Willie had run the unions in the motion picture industry, his friend Gus Greenbaum put him on as Vice President of Entertainment at the Riviera, explaining to his bosses in Chicago that he needed Willie Bioff to negotiate better contracts with the stars. Boss Tony Accardo and the rest of the Chicago group hated Bioff, of course, because it was Bioff's testimony that sent many of Accardo's best people to prison. Tony Accardo wanted Bioff out of the Riviera.

Tony sent Johnny Marshall (Marshall Caifano) to visit with Gus Greenbaum. Marshall was probably the most feared man in Las Vegas!

"Gus, you gotta stop being stupid," said Caifano. "You have to get rid of Willie Bioff, or else. As much as I like you, I'll have to use the torch . . . and I don't want to do that. Gus, you know if I'm told to rub you out, I got no choice, right? Why don't you just get rid of Bioff, you know how it's bothering Accardo!"

In the 1950s and 1960s, Las Vegas was a very safe place to live. The Mob realized that their cash cows, the casinos, would soon go out of business if vacationers were afraid to visit because of Mob violence. So, no one was hit in Las Vegas. If you were wanted by the Mob, and you were lucky enough to escape to Las Vegas, you could live within its confines securely. At that time, there were probably a hundred men who lived in Las Vegas who would have been killed anywhere else in the country. Vegas was a safe haven for Mobsters.

On Nov. 4, 1955, Willie Bioff left the Riviera early and flew on a private plane to his house in Phoenix – he thought secretly. He had to fly back in the morning, though. He had lots to do.

After spending the night at home with the wife and kids, he left real early in the morning. He wanted to get to the airport nice and early. He got into his pickup truck, and pieces of Willie Bioff could be found for days, all over his nice, quiet neighborhood.

Someone had wired five sticks of dynamite to his starter. Although the murder still hasn't been solved, what did come out in the police investigation was that Willie had left Las Vegas along with his friends, Representative and Mrs. Barry Goldwater on the Goldwaters' private plane.

Gus Greenbaum heard about his friend Willie's murder, and it affected him deeply. His drinking and his gambling became more and more frenetic. His womanizing was now being done openly at the Riviera. He began losing more and more money at the Riviera's craps tables, and then he began doing heroin.

He would stay up all night with hookers and not show up in the Riviera lobby until noon the next day. Davie Berman, Gus' friend and Casino Boss, carried much of the load Gus was now neglecting. Then Berman was stricken with cancer and died, and Gus was left without the partner he had depended on for so many years.

The heroin and the drinking began to take their toll. After Gus had gone through the few million dollars he had, he began shortchanging his partners. He began putting money into his pockets.

Marshall Caifano made another trip to the Riviera. He told Gus the Chicago bosses wanted Gus out of the Riviera that very day.

Gus said no, he wasn't goin' nowhere. He knew that he was safe in Las Vegas because no one gets hit in Vegas, although he hired a squad of bodyguards, "just in case." He then went about his gambling and drinking and heroin and whoring until the next morning.

Bess Greenbaum had returned home to Phoenix some months before, and Gus decided to go home to Bess and the family for Thanksgiving. The Greenbaums had a large ranch-style home at 115 No. Monte Vista Road in Phoenix.

The family had a pleasant enough Thanksgiving together. On the morning of Dec. 3, 1958, the Greenbaums' housekeeper, a woman named Pearl Ray, came to work at her regular time and found both Bess and Gus.

Bess was on the living room floor, and Gus was in bed. Their heads were put neatly in plastic bags about 10 feet from their torsos. And since that time, there has not been one other documented case of the Riviera using decapitation as a management tool.

FRANK SINATRA'S CAL-NEVA LODGE

Bones Renner was an old-time gangster from San Francisco. He owned the Cal-Neva Lodge at Crystal Bay on the Nevada side of Lake Tahoe.

But Bones also owed the IRS $800,000 in back taxes. So Bones asked his friend Wingy Grober if he could pass on the ownership of the Cal-Neva. Wingy said "sure," and as a result of his sudden and unexplainable ownership of a casino, ended up with his own set of tax problems. With the IRS after him, Wingy had to put the Cal-Neva Lodge up for sale.

On July 13, 1960, the day John F. Kennedy won the Democratic nomination in Los Angeles, it was announced that Frank Sinatra, Dean Martin, Hank Sanicola, and Sinatra's old friend and business partner from New Jersey, Skinny D'Amato, made application to the state of Nevada to purchase the Cal-Neva.

What wasn't announced in the papers was that Sam Giancana owned Wingy Grober. Wingy was into Sam for a lot of money. So Wingy and Sam made a deal: If Wingy sold the Cal-Neva at a reasonable price to some of Giancana's friends, he'd be off the hook for the money that he owed Giancana.

The reasonable price turned out to be **very** reasonable. The Cal-Neva Lodge was sold in 1960 to Frank Sinatra and associates for $250,000. Everything. The whole place – for 250 Large!

What also didn't make the newspapers about the deal was the FBI assumption that Sinatra was nothing more than a front in the Cal-Neva for New York Mob boss "Fat Tony" Salerno.

As for Giancana's interest in the money-losing casino, he was probably only in the deal to keep next to Sinatra, who was trying, desperately, to keep next to Kennedy, which everybody in the Chicago Outfit wanted.

Dean Martin was involved in the partnership for a very short time. He was told that Giancana was one of the partners, and he decided to bail. Dean's portion of the Cal-Neva was bought by Sandy Waterman. As of Aug. 15, 1961, Nevada records show that Frank owned 36.6 percent of the Cal-Neva. By May 15, 1962, Frank owned 50 percent.

The Cal-Neva was open only from June through Labor Day weekend in September, but Sinatra wanted to make it a year-round operation – it was one of the reasons that he put in the heliport! (No, it doesn't make a lot of sense to me either – but he was quoted a number of times as saying the heliport wasn't just for his buddies – it was for guests, too!)

Sinatra was convinced that the Cal-Neva could produce a hefty profit, and he told Giancana that with the right investment, the place could become a year-round operation.

The Showroom at the Cal-Neva was called the Celebrity Showroom. Sinatra knew acoustics. He had enlarged it to seat 350 – and had it built so he could perform without the need for a microphone. Apparently the acoustics in the Celebrity were as near perfect as you could get in a cabaret. Sinatra opened the first week of June for the three years he owned the place.

To draw attention to the lodge, on opening night, Sinatra's guests included Marilyn Monroe, Joe Kennedy, and his son, John F. Kennedy. Also there that weekend were Johnny Roselli and Sam "Momo" Giancana. Uninvited and hiding up in the hills around the casino lodge was an FBI surveillance team with long-range lenses.

What the agents couldn't see was what went on inside the Cal-Neva's secluded bungalows after the opening night party ended. Momo Giancana reportedly told his brother that he had been present at a Kennedy brothers slumber party that night at the Cal-Neva Lodge. "The men," he said, "had sex with prostitutes – sometimes two or more at a time – in bathtubs, hallways, closets, on floors, almost everywhere but the bed." *(From the Frank Sinatra FBI files)*

Another one of Sinatra's "improvements" was the installation of tunnels – one tunnel was installed between the showroom and Cabin 5, Frank's Cabin – and another between Cabin 3 and Cabin 5.

Three small cabins at the Cal-Neva – 3, 4, and 5 – all next to each other, commanded the premier view of the Crystal Bay portion of Lake Tahoe. When Sinatra came in, he made a rule: Cabin 5 was his, 4 and 3 (and Cabin 50) would never be rented out. Period.

To quote Skinny D'Amato again, "Cabin 3 was for the broads, 4 was for the pals, and 5 was Frank's."

Marilyn Monroe's Cabin 3 at Frank Sinatra's Cal-Neva Lodge.

Marilyn's Cabin

Cabin 3 is probably best known as Marilyn Monroe's Cabin. Although there were many, many women who stayed in Cabin 3 as Sinatra's personal guests, Marilyn's frequent visits there have been well documented.

Over the three years that Sinatra was in charge of the Cal-Neva, Marilyn was reported to be in Cabin 3 while JFK was reported to be in Frank Sinatra's Cabin 5, or Marilyn was reported to be in Cabin 3 while Bobby Kennedy was reported to be in Frank Sinatra's Cabin 5, or Marilyn was reported to be in Cabin 3 while Frank Sinatra was reported to be in Frank Sinatra's Cabin 5.

Lots of FBI and news reports documented Marilyn's comings and goings, including her very last visit to the Lodge – July 27 through July 29, 1962.

She overdosed on pills while in Cabin 3, but managed to call the Reception Desk. Rescue personnel reached her in time, her stomach was pumped, and she survived. She was there that weekend with the Lawfords, Peter and Pat, and possibly Bobby Kennedy, although that's never been proven.

Ten days later on Aug. 5, 1962, she was more successful. Marilyn Monroe was found dead at her home at #5 Helena Drive in Brentwood (California).

A Getaway for the Pals

Cabin 4 was saved for friends. It was used by Deano and Sammy and Vic Damone and Milton Berle and Don Rickles. Skinny D'Amato and his friends stayed there too.

Johnny Roselli stayed in Cabin 4. Ray Patriarca had a key to 4. Jimmy Hoffa loved the place, and didn't want to be seen there. Neither did Carlo Gambino and Paul Costellano, and Aniello Dellacroce – and lots of other friends – men who wanted nothing more than to be able get away from the office for a few days, out in the country where the cops aren't watching you go to the bathroom, a place you can get away from it all. Frank Sinatra's Cal-Neva was perfect.

In 1961, a Chicago hood named Crackers Mendino died of a heart attack. Over the years, he had worked under everyone from Torrio to Giancana in the juke box, pinball, and gambling end of the business. Tony Accardo was one of his pallbearers, and anybody who was anyone in the Chicago Outfit was there for the burial, probably the largest big-time Mob funeral since the days of Al Capone.

At the funeral, Tony Accardo and Sam Giancana had a meeting. They decided they should have someone out at the Cal-Neva to watch over Frank Sinatra. Sinatra was much too enamored with the Kennedys and wasn't thinking straight anymore.

Sam Giancana called Johnny Roselli, who was the Chicago Outfit's man on the West Coast. Anything that needed to be done in Las Vegas or California went through Roselli. When Roselli returned to Las Vegas, he called a hood named Lou McWillie, whom he had first met back in 1938, when Roselli did a short stint as Chicago's rep to the Sans Souci Casino in Havana.

McWillie had worked in Cuba for years, mostly for Meyer Lansky. He was never clear to anyone exactly what it was he did for Lansky, telling the Warren Commission only that he was a key man at Lansky's Tropicana Casino in Havana.

When Castro booted Lansky out of Cuba, Lansky arranged to have McWillie moved into the Tropicana in Las Vegas as a "Casino Executive." Otherwise, there's little known about McWillie, who also used the alias of Lewis N. Martin (apparently, McWillie loved Dean and Jerry). According to the Warren Commission files, the FBI kept him under surveillance and considered him to be a top Mob hit man and enforcer for hire.

Roselli told McWillie that Chicago wanted him out at Sinatra's Cal-Neva Lodge to keep an eye on their investment in the place. And to watch Sinatra and report his activities back to Roselli. McWillie did as he was told and created a job for himself at Sinatra's Cal-Neva, working as a pit boss.

On June 30, 1962, an intoxicated Chuckie English, a Giancana hood, staggered out of the Armory lounge and bumped into one of the FBI agents tagging Giancana. English told the agents that if "Bobby Kennedy wants to know anything about Momo, all he had to do was to ask Sinatra."

The agent reported the conversation back to Hoover who brought the comment to Robert Kennedy's attention, who told Hoover to increase the FBI's surveillance on Sinatra and the Cal-Neva.

The casino was already being investigated because the Feds suspected that the casino's manager, Skinny D'Amato, was running a statewide prostitution ring out of the place. The agents suspected that the women were being flown in from San Francisco with the operation being run openly from the hotel front desk. *(The previous information and quotes from the Frank Sinatra FBI files)*

Deputy Sheriff

Then, a few days after the Chuckie English fiasco, there was the attempted murder of a Cal-Neva employee who was shot on the front steps of the lodge. No one knows if it was Mob-related or not, since the incident was hushed up.

On June 30, 1962, Deputy Sheriff Richard Anderson came to pick up his beautiful brunette wife at the Cal-Neva where she worked as a waitress. The Sheriff's wife had been one of Sinatra's girlfriends for a while before she married Anderson, three months earlier. Anderson had noticed the way Sinatra stared at his wife and heard about the rude and off-color remarks he made to her, so Deputy Anderson, who was twice Sinatra's size, warned the singer to stay away from her. Sinatra backed down and apologized and promised to leave the woman alone.

But Sinatra was a man who brooded and let things build up inside him, and on the night Anderson came to pick up his wife, as he stopped by the kitchen to talk with some of the help there, Sinatra came in, saw Anderson and ran up to him and screamed at him, "What the fuck are you doing here?"

Deputy Anderson remained calm and said he was waiting for his wife, then, suddenly, while the cop was still in midsentence, Sinatra grabbed him and tried to throw him out. After a brief wrestling match, Anderson punched Sinatra so hard in the face that he couldn't perform on stage for a week.

Several weeks later, on July 17, 1962, Anderson and his wife were driving down Highway 28, not far from the Cal-Neva, when they were driven off the road by a late model maroon convertible with California plates, driving at high speed. Anderson lost control of his car, skidded off the road and smashed into a tree, killing him instantly. His wife was thrown from the car and suffered severe broken bones and fractures.

In an interview with a Reno television station, Anderson's mother said, "We still think to this day that Sinatra had something to do with our son's death." Anderson left behind four children.

What a Way to Go

But Sinatra's troubles with the Cal-Neva weren't over yet. A few days after Anderson was driven off the road, and one week before her death, Marilyn Monroe flew to the Cal-Neva at Frank Sinatra's invitation.

Sinatra told Monroe that he wanted to discuss their upcoming film together, *What a Way to Go*. Monroe didn't want to go, but someone told Marilyn that Bobby Kennedy would be there. It sounded logical to Monroe, since it had been in the papers that the Attorney General was in Los Angeles on business.

Sinatra flew Monroe out on his own plane along with Peter Lawford, although Sinatra was no longer speaking to Lawford or Lawford's wife, Patricia Kennedy Lawford.

Exactly what happened that weekend at the Cal-Neva, isn't known and may never be known. Louie McWillie, who was still working for Sinatra at the Cal-Neva, said in a newspaper interview, "There was more to what happened up there than anybody has ever told. It would have been a big fall for Bobby Kennedy."

What is known is that there was a dinner with Momo Giancana and Phyllis McGuire, Peter and Pat Lawford, Frank Sinatra, and Marilyn Monroe.

Momo, of course, had no business being in the Cal-Neva since he was listed in the Nevada Black Book – The List of Excluded Persons, made up of people forbidden to enter a casino. He was at the top of the list of restricted persons, although, as San Francisco's news columnist Herb Caen said, "I saw Sinatra at the Cal-Neva when Sam Giancana was there. In fact I met Giancana through Frank. He was a typical hood, didn't say much. He wore a hat at the lake, and sat in his little bungalow, receiving people" (*San Francisco Chronicle*, June 3, 1962).

Sinatra: "Don't fuck with me."

The McGuire sisters were scheduled to perform at the Cal-Neva. Giancana was dating Phyllis McGuire, with whom he shared a chalet during her performance there.

Unfortunately for Giancana, McGuire, Sinatra, and the Cal-Neva, the FBI photographed the hood playing golf with Sinatra and having drinks and dinner together in the Cal-Neva dining room.

The FBI was also watching that same evening when, during a small party in Dorothy McGuire's room, Victor LeCroix Collins, longtime friend and the road manager of the McGuire Sisters, became irritated when Phyllis McGuire kept walking by his seat and punching him on the arm.

"So I told her," Collins said, "you do that again and I'm going to knock you right on your butt. A half an hour later she punches me again, so I grabbed her by both arms and meant to sit her in the chair I got out of, but I swung around and missed the chair, she hit the floor. She didn't hurt herself, but Sam came charging across the room and threw a punch at me wearing a huge big diamond ring that gouged me in the left eye.

"I just saw red then and grabbed him, lifted him clean off the floor. I was going to throw him through the plate glass door, but thought, why wreck the place? We struggled and got as far as the door, and then I got hit on the back of the head. I don't know who hit me from behind but the back of my head was split open. It didn't knock me out, and as I went down with Sam underneath me, I saw he had on a pearl gray, silk suit, and blood from my eye was running all over it. I had ahold of him by the testicles and the collar and he couldn't move. That's when Sinatra came in with his valet, George, the colored boy. They were coming to join the party, and the girls were screaming and running around like a bunch of chickens in every direction because nobody knew what was going to happen.

"George just stood there with the whites of his eyes rolling around and around in his black face because he knew who Sam was and nobody ever fought with Sam. Sinatra and George pulled me off Sam, who ran out the door" *(verbatim - Sinatra FBI files).*

The next morning, the FBI, which had a fairly clear idea of what had happened the night before, as well as several rolls of film of Sinatra with Giancana, filed its report, with photographs, with the State of Nevada Gambling Control Board. After reading the report, the Control Board's chairman, Ed Olson, called Sinatra at the Cal-Neva and asked about Giancana being on the property. Sinatra said that he saw a man who looked like Giancana and that they just waved and nodded to each other and that was all.

But the FBI also had wind of the fight and sent the investigators to Omaha (where the McGuire Sisters were playing at the Orpheum Theater) to interview Collins.

There was little else Olson could do. Sinatra was a casino owner, with substantial investments in the state, and he was also a major celebrity who was singularly responsible for drawing tens of thousands of tourists into Nevada.

Then the newspapers got hold of the story and backed Olson into a corner, forcing him to remark that his investigation would not conclude until "certain discrepancies in the information provided by various people at Cal-Neva could be resolved."

Sinatra read that and called Olson and asked him to come to the Cal-Neva for dinner "to talk about this, your statements." Olson said that he felt it was inappropriate to be seen at the Cal-Neva having dinner with Sinatra, since the singer was, technically, under investigation by Olson's office, and even if Sinatra weren't under investigation, Olson said, it would still be unacceptable for the Gaming Commissioner to be seen fraternizing with a casino owner.

"But Frank kept insisting," Olson said, "and I kept refusing. The more I refused, the madder he got until he seemed almost hysterical. He used the foulest language I ever heard in my life."

To calm Sinatra down, Olson agreed to meet Sinatra in Olson's office but Sinatra didn't show up. An hour later Sinatra called Olson in a rage. "You listen to me Ed . . . you're acting like a fucking cop, I just want to talk to you off the record."

Olson, in an attempt to take back the high ground that his position required, said: "Who I am speaking to?"

"This is Frank Sinatra! You fucking so-and-so! F-R-A-N-K, Sinatra."

Olson avoided the insults and said that any meeting between them would have to be on record in the presence of witnesses. Sinatra cut him short and screamed, "Now, you listen, Ed! I don't have to take this kind of shit from anybody in the country and I'm not going to take it from you people ... I'm Frank Sinatra!"

Sinatra went on and on, until, at one point, Olson warned Sinatra that if he didn't show up for an interview, Olson would have him subpoenaed. "You just try and find me," the singer threatened, "and if you do you can look for a big fat surprise, a big fat fucking surprise. You remember that, now listen to me, Ed, don't fuck with me. Don't fuck with me, just don't fuck with me" *(verbatim - Sinatra FBI files)*.

"Are you threatening me?" Olson asked.

"No...just don't fuck with me and you can tell that to your fucking board of directors and the fucking commissioner, too."

The next day two investigators came to watch the count at the Cal-Neva. When Sinatra saw them, he yelled across the casino to Skinny D'Amato, "Throw the dirty sons of bitches out of the house. Out of the house."

The agents left before an incident could be started, but came back the next day, only to have D'Amato offer them $100 each "to cooperate." The agents reported the bribe to Olson, who began the steps to revoke Sinatra's license.

When the news was announced that Sinatra was under investigation and would probably lose his casino license, few people in Nevada rushed to his aid. A lot of people resented Sinatra, others despised him, and very few people felt that he should have gotten a state gaming license in the first place. The word around the capitol building in Reno was that Sinatra needed to be taught a lesson.

The lesson they taught him was that they had more power. They took away his license to operate a casino or hotel in Nevada, thus forcing him to sell not only his 50 percent in the Cal-Neva, but also his 9 percent interest in the Sands, about $3.5 million worth of holdings in 1963.

From the Kitty Kelly book, *His Way:* "I talked to Sam (Giancana) the next day," said Joe Shimon, a Washington, D.C., police officer assigned to the Central Intelligence Agency, "and he told me that Sinatra had cost him over $465,000 on Cal-Neva." He said, "That baboon and his big mouth. All he had to do was to keep quiet, let the attorneys handle it, apologize and get a 30- to 60-day suspension. But, no, Frank has to get on the phone with that damn big mouth of his and now we've lost the whole damn place."

Nevada's Governor, Grant Sawyer, stood behind the Gambling Control Board's decision to yank Sinatra's license. However, one day, while the case was still pending, President Kennedy came to the state and was given a caravan parade through the streets of Las Vegas and found himself sitting in the same car with Governor Sawyer. Kennedy turned to

Sawyer, and said, "Aren't you people being a little hard on Frank out here?"

The Governor didn't reply, but later repeated what Kennedy had said to Ed Olson who was startled by the remark. "That's about the highest degree of political pressure you could ever put into the thing," Olson said.

But the Cal-Neva incident was, for the Kennedys, as Peter Lawford said, "The end of old Frankie boy as far as the family was concerned."

During the three years that Frank Sinatra had partnership in the Cal-Neva, friends of his said he was on top of the world. He was a casino owner, which sometimes is even more impressive than being Frank Sinatra.

TEAMSTERS PALACE LAS VEGAS

H is name was Jay Sarno. One of the larger-than-life guys that made Las Vegas the fun city that it is.

If you're about my age, and you stayed or played at Caesars Palace, chances are you've seen Jay Sarno.

From the beginning, the late 1960s, Caesars attracted the wealthier gamblers, guys who came up to Vegas with their golf buddies more often than with their wives and kids in tow. They were all looking for a weekend of fun, drinking, and gambling. Losing a couple of thousand dollars wasn't going to be the worst thing in the world, as long as they had a good time.

Caesars also targeted the big money players, the guys who they could bring in to Las Vegas, the players from around the world with the million-dollar credit lines.

When you came in through the front doors of Caesars, you'd pass two big couches – one on each side. And on those two big couches were six really beautiful girls – three on each couch. They were dressed beautifully and seemed more interested in you than in their girlfriends who were with them.

Nothing overt, but they made eye contact with nearly all the guys who weren't walking into Caesars with luggage under both arms and wearing Bermuda shorts and black socks. Well, maybe a small smile for you when "the missus" was looking for the nearest bathroom, you know, just to be friendly. One of the very nice amenities that Caesars offered to their well-healed clients was the ease of arranging a few hours' companionship.

Of course it went on in all the hotels (that is until that yo-yo Howard Hughes hit Vegas in 1967). You wanted companionship? Readily and easily available. The bellhop, the front desk guy, the hotels didn't make it difficult or embarrassing for you – I mean, this is Vegas, right? Anyway, the most beautiful of the working girls always hung at the front doors of Caesars – and it was, as far as I'm concerned, a fine way to welcome you back to the hotel. It was done with class – quietly, nothing over the top – just some beautiful girls welcoming you, the weary traveler, back to Caesars Palace.

Jay Sarno, bless his soul, thought of lots of small amenities like that, and it made Caesars a big cash cow for a lot of years.

The story starts with Jay Sarno back in the late 1950s. Jay got into the hotel business relatively easily. One night, he met Jimmy Hoffa of the Teamsters at a party in Detroit. They got to talking about Jay's motel business, and Hoffa said that he thought that the Teamsters might be interested in that type of investment.

Sarno's partner was Nate Jacobson. Jacobson, who owned an insurance company in Baltimore, had provided financing for the Cabana Motels. Jay and Nate's motels all had the word *Cabana* in them. To go bigtime, they needed deeper pockets than Jacobson had, and the Central States Teamsters Pension fund had just about the deepest pockets around.

Hoffa put Sarno together with Red Dorfman, the Teamsters "moneyman." Red controlled the money that the

Teamsters lent from their giant Pension Fund. When Jay Sarno said he was looking to expand his motel empire, the Teamsters' money was made available. Sarno's business plan worked. He made a lot of money and repaid the Teamsters Central States Pension Fund their loan and gave both Red Dorfman and Jimmy Hoffa appropriate "thank you" gifts.

And so began the decades long relationship between the Teamsters and Las Vegas.

Red Dorfman retired, but his hand-picked successor, his 25-year-old stepson, Allen, was going to control the Pension Fund in his place.

One day in 1963, Jay Sarno called his friend Jimmy Hoffa in Detroit.

Sarno said he had an idea that was going to make a lot of people a lot of money, and he wanted the Teamsters in from the get-go. So Jay and Jimmy and Allen Dorfman sat down in Jimmy's office in Detroit to discuss Jay's newest idea.

Instead of a motel, Sarno wanted to build a fabulous hotel in Las Vegas, which he wanted to call the Cabana Palace. And in that fabulous hotel, was going to be the most fabulous damn casino in the world, and behind the cages of that fabulous casino were going to be the most fabulous counting rooms that money could buy. And fabulous amounts of money were going to flow through those rooms each day ... you get the drift! Allen Dorfman was impressed with Jay Sarno and with his idea for a Cabana Palace. The name of course was changed to Caesars Palace.

The three guys immediately got along, especially Allen and Jay. They both wore nice, big diamond pinkie rings and $350 slacks. The discussion was successful, and before long the Central States Teamsters were counting Caesars Palace in their column of assets.

The Teamsters put in about $15 million, and Sarno and some other investors came up with $9 million.

Caesars was actually owned by a who's who of the underworld. It's generally thought on the street that the following guys all had a piece of Caesars:

Tony Accardo and Sam Giancana, out of Chicago; Raymond Patriarca, head of the New England LCN (La Cosa Nostra); Jerry Catena, Vito Genovese's aide, also from Chicago; Vincent Alo "Jimmy Blue Eyes," out of New York; and a few lesser known Mobsters. Doris Day was one of the partners in Jay Sarno's Cabanas, and it was rumored she also had points in Caesars.

Total cost of building Caesars came in at $24 million.

Caesars Palace during construction, 1965. The parking lot, on the left side of the Caesars building site, is the only portion that Howard Hughes DID NOT sell to Jay Sarno of Caesars. With the help of Parry Thomas and the Bank of Las Vegas, in 1971, Steve Wynn was able to purchase that narrow strip of property from Hughes. And then Wynn bluffed Caesars into buying it from him at an enormous profit nearly overnight.

By the way, the name Caesars is not spelled with an apostrophe. The official explanation is that Jay Sarno wanted everyone to feel like he was a Caesar, and all Caesars owned it – or something like that. The word on the street was that it was a mistake. Also, there was some disagreement as to where an apostrophe should be. The money had already been spent on the signage, so it was left alone.

Caesars was a monster success from day one. Everyone in on it was happy. Jay Sarno was happy, the Teamsters were happy, the boys in Chicago, and the guests, who were treated royally, were happy.

Sarno lived larger than life, and everything he was involved in with Caesars reflected his lifestyle. The Bacchanal Room was Jay Sarno's personality. While you were eating, beautiful women dressed in gossamer togas would come around and massage your shoulders while you ate. Not your wife's shoulders – this was for the guys at the table only! Had something to do with how Jay Sarno and apparently Caesar thought men should be treated.

Jay Sarno liked to play craps. During his divorce proceedings, he testified in open court that he had lost "between $6 and $7 million dollars" on the craps tables at Caesars.

Speaking of his divorce: Two of my eBay clients, both lovely women, were in Las Vegas during the Jay Sarno years. One worked as a waitress at the Sahara for a number of years and then went over to work at the Caesars Bacchanal Room.

The other was a dancer in the Folies Bergere at the Tropicana, but then became a showgirl at Caesars. Both of these women told me that several of their girlfriends were "seeing" Jay Sarno. Apparently, lots and lots of women "saw" Jay Sarno.

Caesars was amazing. It had more opulence than any other Strip resort, it had fountains and statues and high rollers and the most beautiful call girls in Las Vegas. One thing

Caesars didn't have, however, was a name entertainer in residence.

The fight between Frank Sinatra and Carl Cohen, casino manager at the Sands, worked out perfectly for Sarno.

Howard Hughes didn't like Frank Sinatra. So, Howard Hughes' "people" didn't like Frank Sinatra. Sure, Frank brought in the high rollers, but he was also "very high maintenance."

Hughes decided to get rid of Sinatra, and wanted to insult him in the process. (Both Hughes and Sinatra were after Ava Gardner in the 1940s. Gardner picked Sinatra, and Hughes refused to take it philosophically.) Hughes spoke to Bob Maheu, his assistant, and told him to get rid of Sinatra, and to do it publicly.

Sinatra was a fairly big blackjack player. For years, whatever Mr. Sinatra wanted, Mr. Sinatra got. Credit at the tables went without question, and it was not unusual for Sinatra to sign markers for as much as $100,000 in one night.

Bob Maheu's decision was to cut Frank off from credit at $3,000, and it did exactly what Bob Maheu knew it would do ... it sent Sinatra into a rage. A fight broke out between Frank and Casino Manager Carl Cohen. Really, a fist fight. Frank got decked and left the Sands.

Sinatra stayed away from Vegas for about a year after that, but Sarno and Caesars had been after Sinatra to sign there for many years.

When Sinatra and Sarno began negotiations, Sarno wanted Sinatra's services exclusively. In turn, Sinatra wanted a lot of money ($400,000 a week was the likely figure); his own Caesars-provided bodyguard, in addition to Jilly Rizzo, his longtime, personal bodyguard; and the backing from Caesars for him to reapply for a gaming license as a "key employee" with Caesars.

The reapplication for a gaming license and the backing of Caesars Palace was important to Sinatra. He'd lost connections when he'd lost his license in 1961, and people who knew him knew that it bothered him to have to sell the Cal-Neva and his points in the Sands. He wanted to get back into the game as a casino owner.

Frank's contract began on Nov. 23, 1968.

When Sinatra and Sarno shook hands on the deal, nearly every headliner on the Strip was playing two shows a night and three on Saturday. That's 15 shows a week. Sinatra signed with Caesars but agreed to do only eight shows. He was the only entertainer on the Strip who was doing fewer than 15 shows a week! He was paid $400,000 each and every Friday, and was given $10,000 a day to play with. This wasn't a loan, this wasn't money that showed up on his W-2 form. This was just ten $1,000 chips he was given so he'd have a good time in the casino.

In 1969, Frank Sinatra and the casino manager at Caesars, Sandy Waterman, got into a real fight. Had to do with Sinatra wanting to sign for more chips or something. Doesn't much matter, but Sandy was called over to ask Frank to please quiet down, Frank swung, connected, Sandy swung, they ended up on the floor of the aisle in the high limit room. Sinatra began choking Waterman, Waterman pulled a gun and threatened to kill Sinatra.

Security grabbed the gun out of Waterman's hand, and, believe it or not, Sandy Waterman, casino manager of Caesars Palace, was arrested on the floor of his own casino; first and only time it ever happened in Las Vegas. Well, that's not exactly true, but at the Stardust and the Tropicana, the LVPD had the courtesy to ask the casino managers to step off the floor and out of the eyes of the public before they were arrested.

✳

New Year's Eve, Dec. 31, 1967; the day Evel Knievel jumped over the fountains at Caesars and slid all the way into the Dunes parking lot and into a coma for weeks afterward.

Along came Lum's. Yup, the restaurant people. That Lum's. The owners of Lum's, the Perlman Brothers, offered Jay Sarno $60 million for Caesars Palace. Jay and the Teamsters and a few others had invested about $24 million in it and had it for 34 months – not a bad return! So, they sold! Nothing makes your venture capitalist happier than turning a big profit FAST!

Of course, Allen Dorfman was very happy with Jay Sarno and his "golden touch" and was more than happy to lend Sarno even more money to make his next dream come true – Circus Circus.

FIGHT NIGHT AT THE SANDS

One of Sinatra's last performances at the Sands. c:1967

Carl Cohen, the 288-pound Casino Boss of the Sands

vs.

Frank Sinatra, the 151-pound Legend of the Sands

But first, a little history of the Sands:

1952

Jake Freedman of Texas was the first President of the Sands. The ownership of the Sands is fairly well documented and can be traced to as many as nine different Mob families.

Primary owner would probably have been Doc Stacher, New Jersey Mobster. Jake Freedman, the public face of the Sands – Jakie, as he preferred to be called – was a much loved and respected owner – something that can't be said about a lot of Las Vegas hotel bosses.

Jakie was a genuine Jewish cowboy. He was five foot three, with his high-heeled boots on, and wore a wonderful 10-gallon hat and matching glittering cowboy outfit nearly all the time. Oh, and there was his cologne. Jakie Freedman wore White Shoulders. Yeah, it's women's stuff. But Jake Freedman liked the scent, so Jake Freedman wore White Shoulders, and nobody laughed at him.

There was a very famous craps game at Joe W. Brown's Horseshoe Club. (It had been Binion's Horseshoe Club until Brown purchased it when Benny was sent to jail for tax evasion and some other charges.)

A typical game was described as follows. It started at 11 a.m. Nick the Greek was in, and so were some well-heeled players including Jake Freedman. A sign went up on the table real quick – Minimum Bet $100. No problem for Freedman. He always played with real cash, nothing smaller than a hundred. By midnight, there was over $2 million in chips either on the craps layout or in the racks in front of the players.

When Jake was interviewed later about the game, he said that at one time he was "stuck over a million." But he came back in the early morning hours and walked away from the game having made most of it back.

1956

Jakie Freedman died and the Sands was purchased by two of the legends of early Las Vegas. Both Jack Entratter and Carl Cohen were already running most of the day-to-day operations at the Sands.

Jack Entratter, who co-owned the Copacabana in New York, was hired to manage the entertainment and the showrooms. Good decision – Entratter was friends with everyone who was anyone in show biz, including Walter Winchell, Earl Wilson, Louella Parsons, Hedda Hopper, and other nationally syndicated columnists, all of whom he got to cover the brand new Sands Hotel. It also helped that nearly everyone he wanted to play the Sands had played his Copacabana in New York.

Carl Cohen was a totally respected professional gambler. A pro from the "back end" of the games, he ran the business end of gambling. He knew gamblers, he knew who to keep out of the Sands, and who to make sure was comped for everything imaginable. Also, Carl was a stand-up guy, respected and genuinely liked by his employees as well as his bosses.

When Cohen first came to Las Vegas in the early 1950s, he dealt craps downtown, then was offered the job as Casino Manager at the El Rancho Vegas. But working for Beldon Katleman was not a good experience, so when the Sands opened, Carl jumped at the chance of coming in and taking over the casino.

1967

Howard Hughes bought the Sands for $14.6 million. At the time, the Sands had 777 rooms and nearly 200 acres of land.

Hughes bought the Sands from Carl Cohen and Jack Entratter; the deal was handled by Bob Maheu. The Hughes Organization left Moe Dalitz in place when they purchased the Desert Inn. But Carl Cohen and Jack Entratter both got new bosses at the Sands. The Hughes Group, lawyers, accountants, bean-counters and the like, came in heavy. They began setting down new "rules of operation" – first and foremost, no more casino credit unless all the paperwork was filled out properly.

"Wanna sign a marker for some chips? May I see your driver's license please? Yes, Mr. F., of course I know you, I know you've been a heavy hitter with us for years – but them's the rules, now. I really am sorry."

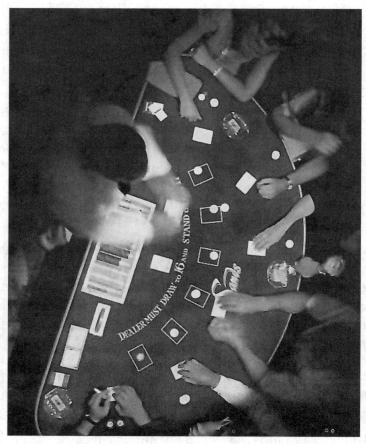

View through "Eye in the Sky"

In the 1950s narrow catwalks were built between vantage points above the tables.

Meanwhile, Howard Hughes didn't like Frank Sinatra. Sure, he brought the high rollers in, but he was also very high maintenance. The two men had a history together. Her name was Ava Gardner.

Years earlier, Ava left Hughes for Sinatra – and Hughes didn't have much of a sense of humor about it. Sinatra found out that Hughes had hired a team of detectives to follow him for nearly a year, reporting his whereabouts to Hughes, who, it was said, also gave the reports on Frank's activities to his friend J. Edgar.

According to Kitty Kelly in her book, *His Way*, when Hughes bought the Sands, Frank said he wouldn't renew his contract until Hughes bought the Cal-Neva Lodge from him. In 1963, when Frank's gambling license was lifted because of his relationship with Momo Giancana, Frank sold his 9 percent of the Sands, but he still owned half of the Cal-Neva Lodge in Lake Tahoe.

He leased the Cal-Neva Lodge to Warner Brothers who had operated it since 1963. He now wanted to cash out, and he figured if Howard wanted him to remain at the Sands, he'd make some money off it. However, Hughes didn't want to buy Sinatra's half of the Cal-Neva and wouldn't even take Sinatra's calls to talk it over on the phone. Sinatra never took rebuke very well. Howard decided to dump Sinatra – and to insult him in the process. The way it was done was to cut off Sinatra's credit.

Fight Night: Sept. 11, 1967

Frank Sinatra sat down at a table in BJ Pit 2 at the Sands. He was scheduled to perform two shows later that night in the Copa Room, the 8 p.m. (Dinner Show), and the Midnight (2 Drink Minimum) Show.

Sinatra was a blackjack player. He sat down and signed for $50,000 in chips. He soon lost it and wanted to sign for another $5K. The dealer knew he couldn't give it to Mr. S, so he called over the pit boss, Ed Walters. Ed was a real old-time gambling boss at the Sands – a guy who knew how to run a blackjack pit. He was just told by his boss, Carl Cohen, that Sinatra's credit is no more at the Sands. Walters apologized, "We just can't Mr. S."

Sinatra went crazy, screaming, cursing. "Where the hell is Jack [Entratter]? That Jew bastard Carl [Cohen] is trying to fuck with me again." Apparently, it didn't occur to Frank that instructions to cut off his credit came from much higher up.

There are two good stories here. Both versions place the scene in the Garden Terrace, the great Sands coffee shop, right off the pool.

Version 1 (the one I like) is that Frank went outside by the pool, looking for someone to tell him where Jack or Carl were, so he could "get this bologna straightened out." He saw Carl Cohen sitting at a table in the Garden Terrace with two other men. Sinatra grabbed one of those neat electric golf carts that the bellboys used to transport guests and their luggage to one of the back buildings, and he drove the golf cart through the plate glass window right at Carl.

Version 2 has Frank just pushing his way through the waiting line ranting and screaming curses at Carl who was seated in the coffee shop.

From here, both versions converge. There's lots of yelling and cursing, then Frank picks up a chair and throws it at Carl – not hitting him, by the way. Carl Cohen was a big man, both physically, over 300 pounds, and in his connections in Las Vegas. He ran the entire casino operation at the Sands. A very competent, real tough casino boss. Sinatra had stepped over the line. Carl swung and knocked Sinatra to the ground, busting out the bridgework of his front teeth.

Frank may have expected some back up from Jilly Rizzo, his driver, bodyguard, and pal, but Jilly wasn't about to go against Carl Cohen. He helped Frank up, and they went out past the pool, to Sinatra's private and secluded three-bedroom stand-alone suite. They packed up and drove to McCarran, then flew back to Frank's Bel Air home. (Frank's wife at the time, Mia Farrow, hardly ever went to Las Vegas. She lived in their Bel Air or Palm Springs home.) It would be many years before Frank Sinatra set foot in the Sands again.

The Sands was a small hotel. Word of the fight spread around the hotel quickly, and within the hour, everyone, employees as well as guests, were aware of what happened. After dinner had been cleared away, and right before the show was about to start (Alan King had been found to replace Sinatra), suddenly, some of the waiters turned to the back of the room and began applauding. Then, everyone else began applauding. Curious guests didn't know who the big man leaving the showroom was, but Carl Cohen had become a hero, at least with the people who worked at the Sands. There was a poster of Sinatra that someone had put up in the dealers' breakroom. Someone had blackened out his two front teeth and written across the bottom *Carl Cohen for President.*

A year later, Sinatra began headlining at Caesars, where he also had a sweet deal and drove the employees crazy.

HOW TO CHEAT A FRIAR

Phil Silvers and Zeppo Marx left the Friars Club on Santa Monica Boulevard together that night.

While they were waiting for Zeppo's white Rolls to be brought out front, they both lamented on another very expensive evening of gin rummy. "I really got hurt tonight," Silvers said.

On the third floor of the club was a windowless and very elegant card room. Dark wood, deep comfortable chairs, a self-service bar with good liquor, snacks, and sandwiches, and three card tables.

Zeppo had been playing against Vic Lands – Dr. Victor Lands, 53, was a Beverly Hills physician whose patients were mostly celebrities and the ultra-wealthy of Beverly Hills.

Silvers was playing against Maury Friedman, as he did most nights. Maury was a real estate developer in both LA and on the Las Vegas Strip. Most of the Friars thought that he was "with the Mob." Not that big a deal really; there were lots of money folks who belonged to the club from show business, movie studios, unions, Las Vegas. Being "with the Mob" wasn't unusual.

"It's the damnedest thing," Zeppo was saying. "For years now, I've been on a cold streak over here. At Hillcrest I do just fine, but here I lose my shirt, night after night!"

Hillcrest was the Country Club over on Pico Boulevard. Big gin game there six nights a week. The regulars at the Hillcrest game were Zeppo's brother, Groucho; Jack Benny; Joe Schenk, a producer at Paramount; Milton Berle; Louie B. Mayer, and that crowd.

Phil Silvers felt the same way as Zeppo did. He used to play a pretty decent game of gin. He'd win a few hundred, lose a few hundred; he kept even. "But these last two or three years, I've been losing some very serious money to guys I used to beat all the time. And do you know what's really strange?" said Silvers. *"Everyone I've spoken to who's played against Maury Friedman has had that same feeling, that somehow he was cheating. But how do you cheat at gin?"*

The valet brought Zeppo's Rolls convertible around, Zeppo said goodnight to his longtime friend, and drove away. Across the street, the FBI had been watching the two men, and as Zeppo was pulling away, they noticed that on the roof of the Friars Club, a man in a gray jumpsuit had just climbed out of a trap door and down a ladder on the side of the building.

They watched him go around a corner getting as many photos of him as they could, but they weren't going to follow him. That wasn't their assignment that night. The FBI guys would write up a full field report in the morning on what sure looked suspicious, but tonight they went back to watching the front door. They were waiting for Johnny Roselli to leave.

This was 1967, and Johnny Roselli was being tailed. It was well known that Roselli was now the Mob boss of Las Vegas – but he was absolutely professional, and no matter how much

J. Edgar wanted to get Roselli, the FBI had turned up nothing.

Then quite by accident, while working on another case, the FBI had found out through an informer that Johnny Roselli's real name was Fillipo Sacco.

And finally, J. Edgar had something he could use on Johnny Roselli.

When Roselli came to the US in the 1920s, his name was Fillipo Sacco, but after he joined the Mob and migrated to Chicago, he left the name behind in Boston, along with his mother and brother. Maybe Fillipo Sacco sounded too Italian, how about Giusseppe Roselli? There's a good American name! His friends called him Johnny.

So, Fillipo Sacco had a nice birth certificate made up, and a driver's license in his new name, and transformed into Johnny Roselli, Mob enforcer.

He did such a fine job in his first years, he caught the eye of some of the real power in the Mafia, men like Tony Accardo and Paul Ricca who were the top two men in the Chicago Outfit, and Frank Costello, head of one of the Five Families in New York.

Tony Accardo sent Roselli to Los Angeles "to take care of the Mob's interests in the movie business." He did a wonderful job enforcing what Chicago wanted enforced in Hollywood.

Roselli believed in discussing a problem first, then explaining the problem, and if cooperation wasn't quick enough, or if it was necessary to apply pressure, well, two button men, Hooky Rothman and Aldiano Frattiano, the two best contract killers in the world, were on Roselli's payroll. Frattiano was much better known in later years as Jimmy "the Weasel." But, that was later – when he turned into a squealer.

Even in his early days in Hollywood, Roselli had "juice." Roselli could start a strike on a movie set, or he could make sure a strike never happened.

He was connected with most of the major Mobs in the country, all of whom seemed to trust him. And with good cause – Roselli was a man of his word, a standup guy, and everyone knew it.

Johnny Roselli and Harry Cohn, President of Columbia Pictures, became good friends. People who knew about the friendship thought it unusual, because nobody was friends with Harry Cohn. He was possibly the most hated man in Hollywood. But Johnny Roselli knew being friends with the head of a major studio was smart, and Harry Cohn knew that being friends with a very bright, up-and-coming major Mobster was smart. Especially a Mobster who looked like a movie star, had impeccable manners, and lots of style.

The two men liked each other's company. Many movie people thought that Roselli was Cohn's bodyguard, but they were friends. They used to go down to Cohn's home in Palm Springs on the weekends, with a few starlets from Columbia or some of Roselli's girl friends.

Harry owned only a third of Columbia Pictures. Though he was in charge of production, it was his brother Jack Cohn who controlled the purse strings and also owned a third of the studio. The last third was owned by a man named Joe Brandt.

The two brothers, Harry and Jack, didn't speak to each other. When business had to be discussed, they made sure that there was always a stenographer present, who also acted as witness to what was being said. It was that kind of family partnership.

In the early 1930s, the movie studios were doing well. People needed the diversion of movies to take their minds off the Depression.

Columbia Pictures was doing extremely well, and Joe

Brandt knew he could make a lot of money by cashing in now, when money was in such scarce supply. A few hundred thousand dollars would be a lifelong windfall for him and his family. He knew whichever brother he sold his stock to, that brother would have absolute vice-grip control over Columbia Pictures.

So Brandt sat the two brothers down in his office and said, "Guys, I want out – but I want out with a half million dollars in cash. My third of Columbia stock is now for sale. The first one of you who puts $500,000 in my hand, has my stock."

Now, this was 1932. Many of the banks, even the big ones were failing. Jack Cohn called his friend at the Morgan Bank in New York. "Yes, J.P., of course, I know I'm waking you! I need a half million dollars tonight in cash. I'll put up two-thirds of Columbia as collateral!"

It was a good investment for the bank, thought Jack Cohn. Columbia Pictures was expected to make over $5 million profit this year. However, the Morgan president whom he called at 1:30 a.m., didn't think it was a good loan; $500,000 to put into a motion picture studio was way too much of a gamble.

"Thanks, but we're just not interested at this time, Jack. Good luck, I hope you get it," he replied, at about 2 a.m.

Chase Manhattan's president was the second to turn down Jack Cohn a little before 4 a.m., as did three other New York bankers he woke up that night.

Meanwhile, Harry Cohn called Johnny Roselli the moment he got back to his office.

Roselli answered Cohn's midnight phone call and immediately came awake.

Cohn: "Johnny, I need a half million dollars quick. You've been looking for an opportunity for your friends to get into the motion picture business. Well, this is it!"

Roselli: "How soon do you need it, Harry?"

Cohn: "Tomorrow and no later. And Johnny, it has to be cash."

Roselli: "I'll get back with you in 15 minutes, Harry. Is that OK?"

Johnny Roselli called New Jersey Mob boss, Abner "Longy" Zwillman. Zwillman sent the $500,000 in $100 bills by plane by 9 a.m. the next morning.

Columbia Studios now belonged to Harry Cohn, with a small piece belonging to "Longy" Zwillman, and a very small piece belonging to Johnny Roselli, who got a small piece of every deal he put together.

To Zwillman and Roselli, this was just a regular business deal. This is what they did. To Harry Cohn, it cemented a lifelong friendship with Johnny Roselli, and it gave him the pleasure of kicking his brother Jack out of Columbia Pictures.

And the Mob got its first toehold into Hollywood, in 1932, with the $500,000 loan to Harry Cohn of Columbia.

In 1951, Columbia Pictures announced it was casting for the movie *From Here to Eternity*. Frank Sinatra desperately wanted the part of Maggio; he knew it would resurrect his career. But Harry Cohn hated Sinatra and swore he'd never get any part in His movies!

Frank Sinatra contacted his friend Frank Costello and asked for help. Costello contacted Johnny Roselli and asked him to talk to Harry Cohn; no one could talk to Harry Cohn except Johnny Roselli.

There was no one else that Harry Cohn would have listened to. Among other things, Roselli told him about the "undying friendship that this would give you with the New York family."

Sinatra was given the role of Maggio and won an Academy Award for Best Supporting Actor of 1953, and now Roselli had a lifelong friend in Frank Sinatra.

[Fast forward: In the *Godfather*, Jack Waltz, head of Waltz Pictures, had to wake up to Khartoum's head in his bed before he gave Johnny Fontaine the part.]

Johnny Roselli was described by people who knew him as courtly, gentlemanly, Old World. He was courteous, and he dressed elegantly. His hair had gone prematurely white some years before; he was known to his friends as the "Silver Fox." Roselli was friendly with everyone. His friends were the Mafia Dons from the various families around the country, studio heads, actresses, and millionaires of Beverly Hills.

Roselli bought into some of the better Hollywood restaurants, where he entertained his friends, the movers and shakers in Hollywood. It was a good life that Johnny Roselli had, however, he never forgot why he was there – to make sure that the unions who were servicing the motion picture industry did right by the studios. Also, Johnny Roselli was one of the Mob's leading loan sharks on the West Coast. But only large amounts, and only famous clients.

Johnny Roselli was out to protect the Mob's businesses, and the motion picture studios were certainly the Mob's business. Over the years, Roselli did so well for the Chicago Outfit and the other Mobs he represented in LA, that a new role opened up for him.

In early 1957, he was told to pack up and move to Las Vegas. Johnny, who loved Las Vegas, packed up and moved. He took one apartment at the Desert Inn and another on Paradise Road. He'd represented Chicago's interest in Las Vegas for a short while in the early 1950s. Again, his responsibility was to keep watch out for Chicago's interests, and he was so good at it that soon he was looking out for the interests of other Mob families. He became the Outside Man in Vegas for nearly everyone.

Within a year, he was instrumental in getting construction financing for the Tropicana, the Royal Nevada, and for expansion of a few Strip hotels. His source of money was usually the Teamsters Central States Pension Fund, which was controlled by Chicago mobster Paul "Red" Dorfman, and later by his son Allen Dorfman. Both of these men took orders from Johnny Roselli.

According to the authors Charles Rappleye and Ed Becker in their book *All American Mafioso*, in 1958, Roselli recruited a paid informant who worked in the Las Vegas Sheriff's Department. This guy could access all the sensitive files. Although this was standard procedure for the Mob throughout the country, this was the first time that a leak had occurred in the Las Vegas Sheriff's Department.

By 1959, Roselli was the ranking Mafioso in Las Vegas, and he knew in advance what the FBI was doing. Johnny Roselli was in on nearly every major transaction that took place on the Strip.

From his apartment at the Desert Inn, though his name was never on a letterhead, he controlled the powerful Monte Presser Talent Agency. For quite a few years in the 1960s, nearly all the major performers who played Las Vegas were booked through Johnny's Monte Presser Agency.

Roselli had a wonderful knack of putting people together. That was probably Roselli's most valuable asset. Through all his Los Angeles and Las Vegas years, there was no one better at putting the right people together, whether it was for social reasons, like introducing John F. Kennedy to Judy Exner, who was to become his mistress for some years; or for business, like arranging for Mob friends who had a lot of money to meet with casino builders who sure could use a lot of money.

The developers of the Royal Nevada, the Frontier, the Dunes, and the Aladdin were all matched up with Mob guys. And Roselli got a piece of everything he was involved in. Every time he made something happen, he became stronger and stronger in the Mob hierarchy. And nearly every self-respecting Mob family in the country had investments in Las Vegas – investments that Johnny Roselli had gotten them into. He was highly protective of his clients, and they knew it.

Enter Maury Friedman

While Maury Friedman lived in LA in the 1940s and 1950s, he made a fortune in land speculation and real estate development. He belonged to all the best clubs, Hillcrest Country Club and the Friars Club, and played gin rummy at both of them.

Maury Friedman and Johnny Roselli were friends. They'd been involved together in a few business deals, like the financing and building of the New Frontier in 1955. Friedman bought up land and developed hotels. He owned the land the Silver Slipper Casino sat on, and he was involved with a brand new project in Las Vegas, one that needed money – quiet, outside money.

One morning after breakfast, Maury and Johnny got to talking about LA, and the discussion got around to the Friars Club.

Roselli had been a guest there many times, and he was friendly with more than half the Friars who belonged. Maury was a member, had been for years, and Friedman asked Roselli if he'd be interested in joining the Friars. Johnny said, "Sure."

Maury sponsored Roselli; and two of Roselli's good friends, Dean Martin and Frank Sinatra, seconded his nomination to the Friars. Georgie Jessel, who founded the Friars Club, also eased the path for Johnny Roselli's membership. And Roselli and Georgie Jessel became good friends.

Maury Friedman was a pretty fair gin rummy player. He was a wealthy man, just as were the other Friars, and they played for some hefty stakes. But Maury had an idea. One night, like a bolt of lightning, it hit Maury – the eye in the sky, just like in Las Vegas, with a little more sophistication. That was it! That was just what Maury wanted to do in the Friars Club in LA.

So he put together his group, and just like in *Ocean's Eleven*, Maury had the guys over to his house in Beverly Hills to lay out his plan.

Present at the first meeting of the conspirators:

Maury Friedman: Developer, part owner of the Frontier Hotel in Las Vegas

George Search: Electronics wizard, very familiar with the eye in the sky

Vernal Furlong: Electronics wizard, worked for the New Frontier

Al Mathes: Hollywood restaurateur, millionaire

Ed Beghardt: Electronic engineer from Miami

Ben Teitelbaum: Manufactured movie equipment, millionaire

TW Richardson: Owner of The Silver Slipper, now with the Frontier

Ricky Jacobs: Owner of a Santa Monica card club, millionaire

Dr. Victor Lands: Beverly Hills physician with show business clients, millionaire

The Plan: Maury would have the three card tables at the Friars Club wired with good "peeper" cameras. These cameras would be placed in the ceiling, with a catwalk built in so that one of the conspirators could sit up there and peek through the TV camera, enlarging the image until the cards that Maury Friedman's opponent had could be seen. And then, through a remote electronic device strapped to Friedman's torso, a simple code, similar to Morse Code, would be tapped out, and Maury or whoever was getting the help, would play accordingly.

Ricky Jacobs, besides being the owner of a Santa Monica card club, was also a professional gambler. Dr. Lands flew up to Las Vegas at least once a month and was comped wherever he wanted to stay. He was a big player, as was his friend and neighbor in Beverly Hills, Ben Teitelbaum. TW Richardson and Maury Friedman had been business partners and confederates in a good number of Las Vegas and Los Angeles building projects.

Each of these players could play whenever he wished; notification would just have to be made in advance, so that one of the two "spotters," either George Search or Vern Furlong would be up in the ceiling.

The electronics were delivered, unpacked, and hooked up. Over the space of two weeks, usually in the early hours of the morning, a set of pinholes were drilled into the ceiling over the card tables. The cameras and the electronics were installed. The men met 20 or more times to learn the codes, to make sure all the equipment was working properly, and to work out any bugs in the system. Finally they were ready to go.

The first night the game was "fixed," Maury was playing against Harry Karl. Karl was Debbie Reynolds' husband, a millionaire in his own right, and the owner of Karl's Shoes. He loved high-stakes gin games, the higher the better. All of a sudden, Maury Friedman, whom he'd been playing with for years, started getting really hot and called Karl a "chicken" if he didn't want to double the stakes.

Then, with four of his co-conspirators casually hanging around the Friars card room, Friedman took Harry Karl for $30,000! Within two years, Harry Karl was broke. Gambling with Maury Friedman and the other card players at the Friars cost him his business, his money, and his family.

Harry Karl was not alone. Many others lost fortunes to Maury Friedman. Few ever discussed it.

One night, Milton Berle, a friend of Roselli's called him and said, "Johnny, I've been gambling for 50 years. I don't know how, but I'm being cheated by Maury Friedman. Can you help me find out for sure?"

Johnny said he'd look into it, and he did it the most direct way possible. The next morning he drove to LA and went right over to see Maury. Johnny asked him if he were cheating at the Friars Club games.

Maury smiled, and explained the entire set up to Roselli. He even asked Johnny if he'd like to join the group and pick up some easy money.

Roselli wasn't much of a card player, but this was Beverly Hills, and Beverly Hills was his turf. This cheating should not have been done without his knowing about it. So Johnny Roselli gave the Mob-approved answer: "I won't say anything to anybody, Maury, but this is my territory, and from now on, we're partners!" Johnny told Milton Berle he couldn't find any cheating at the club.

This was big-time gin. $10 a point gin. Very serious gin. And it was a fun game to watch. Maury Friedman just kept winning and winning and winning.

That night in February 1967, when Zeppo and Phil Silvers were leaving the Friars Club, they were being watched from across the street by the FBI Task Force charged with tailing Johnny Roselli. The agents weren't that interested in the two movie stars standing in front of the Friars, but that guy climbing out of the trap door, that was something else again. After checking with the Agent-in-Charge of the Los Angeles FBI Office, they got the go-ahead for the very next night to enter the Friars Club by this same trap door to see what was going on.

It didn't take the two trained FBI agents 15 minutes to uncover all of the pinholes, cameras, and trace nearly all of the communication equipment. They wrote a full report on it.

When the report reached J. Edgar's desk, he really didn't think that a few millionaire Friars cheating a few other millionaire Friars at cards was something that the FBI should allocate its resources to. After all, they were there to tail Roselli.

Hoover had learned Roselli was an unregistered alien, and that his documentation in Chicago, his birth certificate, and so on, were just good forgeries. It would be the immigration thing that Hoover could use to finally get rid of Johnny Roselli. And that would have taken our story in an entirely different direction, but Beldon Katleman entered the picture.

Katleman owned the El Rancho Vegas, until it burned to the ground in June 1960. He did very well with the fire. A nice, healthy fire sometimes is just the economic shot-in-the-arm a business owner needs. So much easier than trying to sell a business that had seen better days.

Word on the street has always been that shortly after the fire, Katleman got a "visit" at his home in Las Vegas. He decided that it would be prudent to take his few million dollars, and the big, fat insurance settlement check, and move full time to Los Angeles.

Beldon lived in a beautiful mansion in Bel Air, not far from the Friars Club in Beverly Hills. He ate at the Friars once or twice a week, but he was always a loner there.

Most of the Friars' knew him well, and they were not his friends. But he got involved with the conspirators. And he learned about the ceiling. He loved the idea of having electronic devices that could feed him information in gin games.

He called Johnny Roselli, and asked him if whoever fixed up the Friars card room could also do the card room in his Bel Air mansion. Roselli arranged it, and $11,000 later, Katleman had his own eye in the sky.

The FBI knew that Katleman liked to brag; he liked to name names. An FBI agent named George Bland was asked to befriend Katleman. George went over on some "official business"; he needed to ask Katleman something about his Las Vegas days. And Beldon was happy to talk to Bland.

Over the next few weeks, Beldon Katleman and George Bland began having lunches together. One night, Bland was over at Katleman's having dinner when the FBI agent confided in Katleman that there was electronic cheating going on in the Friars Club card room. He told Katleman that the FBI knew about the cheating, but since their interest was Johnny Roselli, and apparently he wasn't mixed up in the cheating, they ignored what was going on in the club.

And wonderful Beldon Katleman replied, "He isn't mixed up in it? Ha! Of course he's mixed up in it! He doesn't play gin, but gets his share from the take."

Bland shook Katleman's hand. Johnny Roselli, Mob boss of Las Vegas, was about to be busted. Thanks to Beldon Katleman.

The FBI investigation of the Friars Club lasted five months. In that time, the FBI spoke to four of the conspirators and four of the conspirators' lawyers, explaining to them that they weren't interested in prosecuting these four guys. They wanted the men behind the scam – especially Johnny Roselli.

The four men who had already had many meetings with the FBI were granted full immunity if they turned state's evidence and told the FBI everything they knew. Granted immunity from prosecution in exchange for their sworn testimony were George Search and Vernal Furlong, the two "spotters"; Al Mathes, the Beverly Hills restaurant owner; and Ed Beghardt, the electronics engineer from Miami, who rigged the wiring.

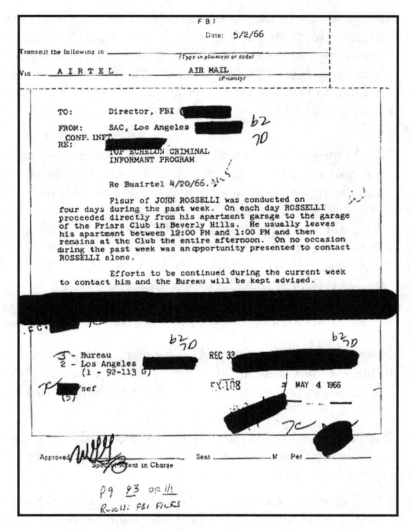

FBI report on surveillance of Johnny Roselli.

On July 20, 1967, two unmarked, white FBI cars pulled up in front of the Friars Club on Santa Monica Boulevard. It was 8:30 in the evening. Armed with arrest warrants as well as search warrants, the FBI men arrested five of the six conspirators that night inside the Friars Club. The sixth defendant, TW Richardson, was being taken into custody by the Las Vegas Sheriff's office at his apartment at the Frontier Hotel.

That same night Los Angeles police called on the homes of 20 Friars – men they knew were in the rigged games, and men they knew had been taken for huge amounts of money. Of all the men who were questioned about their losses, only four were willing to come forward, admit that they were duped, and were willing to talk in court about how much they had lost.

The biggest loser in the group was Debbie Reynolds' husband Harry Karl. He figured that he had lost nearly $1 million in the rigged games, as well as losing his business and family. He was willing to testify at the trial. Phil Silvers, Zeppo Marx, and singer Tony Martin also admitted to hundreds of thousands of dollars in losses in the five years the "Eye in the Sky" had been in operation. They were so angry with Friedman and Roselli that they were eager to testify.

Named as defendants and indicted the next morning were:

Maurice H. Friedman, 62, Las Vegas. A packager of multimillion dollar Nevada hotel deals since the early 1950s, planner, builder and developer of the $25-million Frontier Hotel.

Manuel "Ricky" Jacobs, 48, Beverly Hills. Identified by US Attorney Matt Byrne as a professional gambler and owner of a Santa Monica card club.

Dr. Victor G. Lands, 53, Beverly Hills. A physician practicing in Beverly Hills. His practice seemed to be limited to wealthy show business and music industry people.

Benjamin J. Teitelbaum, 53, Hollywood. Co-owner of a firm that made movie studio equipment, and owner of an art collection valued [in 1962] at $3 million.

T. Warner "TW" Richardson, 62, Las Vegas. Former owner of a Biloxi, Miss., hotel, and operator of Las Vegas' Silver Slipper Casino, now associated with the Frontier Hotel.

Fillipo Sacco, 52, Las Vegas and Beverly Hills. Mr. Sacco is known in Hollywood and Las Vegas as Johnny Roselli.

The US Attorney said all defendants except Richardson were members of the Friars Club, "a charity-and-fun fraternity for the wealthy of show business and its fringes."

During the trial, Friars George Burns, Groucho Marx, George Raft, Milton Berle, Dean Martin – a total of nearly 50 men were served with subpoenas to appear. They appeared, but with the exception of Harry Karl, Tony Martin, Phil Silvers, and Zeppo Marx, none of the other big-time gamblers at the club would even admit to playing once with Johnny Roselli. A few said they weren't even sure who he was!

If only George Search, the guy who had actually installed the electronics equipment, could be taken care of before the trial, chances were Roselli could walk. Search was small time, but he was pivotal in the government's case against Roselli and the rest.

Roselli called a meeting in his lawyer's office in LA. He knew that the FBI couldn't use anything they got from that meeting; it fell under attorney/client privilege.

Maury Friedman was at the meeting, as were Roselli and button men Jimmy Fratianno and Frank "Bomp" Bompensiero. Friedman gave Roselli an envelope with $2,000 in it for expense money for the hit men.

What Roselli and Friedman didn't know was that Bompensiero was already a government informant, and he wore a wire to this meeting.

Jimmy "the Weasel" Fratianno was facing a conspiracy trial the next week, but a nice hit, in the middle of the day? Can't beat it! Fratianno, through his network, knew that tonight George Search was checked in at the Sands Hotel in Las Vegas.

Fratianno flew up to Vegas and spotted Search at one of the 21-tables. Fratianno called Bomp and told him that it was going to be easy. George Search had checked into the Sands under his own name.

Bomp said he'd drive up to Las Vegas later that day. Bomp then told his FBI handler about the contract that Roselli had put on George Search. Later that night, two men from the Las Vegas FBI office went to Search's room at the Sands and told him that Fratianno was already there, and Bomp was on his way. George was going to be hit that night or the next day, right in the hotel.

Search left immediately with the two FBI men and entered into the Federal Witness Protection Program. The chance to get Search was gone.

On May 24, 1968, the trial began in Los Angeles. Throughout the summer and fall of 1968, Johnny Roselli arrived every day at the courthouse in his limousine, wearing another $1,500 suit, and beautifully combed hair. And throughout the six months of the trial, court observers reported, Roselli never cracked a smile.

Roselli was a tough guy. That image was important to him. As an Old World Mafioso, being tough and being quiet was what counted. On Dec. 2, 1968, after 20 hours of deliberation, the jury found all five defendants guilty on all counts.

In the appeal, Roselli's attorney argued before US District Court Judge William Gray that most of the evidence against his client was gathered through years of illegal FBI wiretaps.

He also presented in court character reference letters lauding Johnny Roselli. Besides all the show business personalities and Las Vegas casino owners who wrote the judge telling him what a "standup" guy Johnny Roselli was, even Georgie Jessel, who, in spite of the card cheating at "his" club, wrote the judge that Roselli was "sincere, honest, and one of the best Friars, believe me!"

On Feb. 4, 1969, the court handed down prison sentences to the two main defendants:

Maury Friedman: Six years in a federal penitentiary and a $100,000 fine

Johnny Roselli: Five years in a federal penitentiary and a $55,000 fine, plus six months for his immigration violations – sentences to run concurrently

With the conviction, Johnny Roselli's days in Las Vegas were over, although his days in court were not. Roselli was involved in another great story – The Mob Takeover of the Frontier.

HOWARD HUGHES BUYS NEVADA

On Tuesday, May 3, 1966, Howard Hughes was given a check for $546,549,771.00. (That's five hundred and forty-six million dollars and change.) Add the five hundred and forty mil to what he already had, and he became the richest man in the United States.

Doing some quick calculations – it comes to $85,000 in interest each and every day for the rest of his life. Doesn't much matter what league you play in, that's a lot of money. What does one do with all that money? That's exactly what the IRS was wondering also.

The half billion dollars was about to be taxed. It was considered dormant income, cash not being used, and that's taxed by Uncle Sam at a much higher rate than is working or active income. But the problem for Hughes was, what in the heck can you buy for a half billion dollars in 1966?

"I know! Why don't I go to Vegas for a while. I always enjoy going there."

And so began The Death Knell for the Sands Hotel.

Back in the 1940s, Hughes stayed at the old El Rancho Vegas, which was run by guys he knew and was friendly with. Wilbur Clark had it just after the war, and Howard and Wilbur got along. Conrad Hilton and his wife Zsa Zsa had it during the war. They'd been friends for years. But he and Beldon Katleman, who had inherited the place from his uncle in 1950, just didn't like one another. Hughes was a big-time gambler, and Katleman would always lift the house limit when Howard was at a table. It was said that at blackjack, Howard bet as much as $100,000 per hand. But he was a poor gambler, and that made Beldon Katleman gleeful. When you're losing, whatever the amount is, it's probably counterproductive for employees to laugh at you. Especially the casino owner.

So Howard began spending his weekends up the road at the Last Frontier. He knew Griffin, the owner, pretty well; they were both in the motion picture business in Hollywood. Eventually, Howard took out a long-term lease on one of the suites at the Last Frontier. It was always vacant and ready for him. He also took a suite at the Flamingo, where he stayed for nearly six months.

Hughes also owned the Green Valley Ranch. He bought it from Vera Krupp (ex-actress, married into the Krupp Ironworks money), who needed to sell after being "taken advantage of" by her partners in the Frontier. Hughes never set foot on the property. Too bad, he probably would have been comfortable there.

His standard attire at the casinos included tennis sneakers and an old, wrinkled, light seersucker jacket. He was really scraggly looking. When he walked through a casino, people thought he was a hobo, until they noticed the bodyguards.

If Howard saw a woman he was interested in, he'd send one of his bodyguards or one of the casino executives over to the woman. She was told that Howard Hughes was interested in her company. "Yes, that *is* him over there. It's kind of like a disguise."

And if she was interested in having dinner with the richest single man in the United States, "Please sign this 'hold harmless agreement,' and one of Mr. Hughes' limousines will be out front waiting for you." By the end of the evening, sometimes there were three or four women waiting for Howard in his apartment at the Last Frontier or in the three-bedroom suite at the Flamingo.

However, more often than not, he'd forget about the women and end up doing something else that evening. He was very good about sending expensive gifts the next day, though. Howard was very popular in Las Vegas.

At Thanksgiving time in 1966, Hughes came to Las Vegas by train. He was met by Johnny Roselli and Bob Maheu when the train stopped to let him off outside of town. As had been arranged, the guys took Hughes to the DI secretly, where he occupied the entire ninth floor. The Mormon Mafia, as Hughes' men were called, occupied the eighth floor.

Moe Dalitz and Ruby Kolod, owners of the Desert Inn, had a problem.

Howard Hughes had rented the top two floors of the hotel, which housed all the high-roller suites. New Year's Eve was just around the corner, and the Players Championship Golf Tournament was just around the corner. There were three Whales who were expected and 10 to 15 Premium Players who were expected, and Howard Hughes had the top two floors. Sure, he was playing rent – $26,000 a day – but he didn't gamble.

And the Mormon Mafia didn't gamble, and $26,000 a day ain't nothin' to any of the 60 or 70 people who just weren't going to stay at the Desert Inn if "my regular damn suite ain't available."

Bob Maheu, ex-FBI and Hughes' righthand man, ran Summa Corporation, the holding company for all of Hughes' Nevada businesses. Maheu was being leaned on heavily by Dalitz and Ruby Kolod to get Hughes the heck out of the hotel, or "we're gonna' go up there and throw him out!"

However, his boss, Hughes – the guy who was paying him $10,000 a week (that's $520K a year – in 1967) and giving him an absolutely unlimited expense account, private use of his own jet, a mansion to live in right on the Desert Inn golf course, and a pretty good health and dental policy, also – was telling him over the phone, "Bob, I'm happy here. I like it. Get this resolved for me, will you?"

[Author's note: Although Maheu was making a half million plus in salary, Hughes' long-time executive assistant, Noah Dietrich, was being paid only $75,000 a year.]

So, Bob Maheu called his buddy Johnny Roselli, who had an apartment right there in the Desert Inn. Roselli was operating the most successful booking agency in Las Vegas right out of his apartment, Monte Presser Productions. Maheu explained the problem.

Roselli was the Las Vegas enforcer for the Chicago Outfit. But once in Las Vegas, his real talents came out. He was great at putting things together – people, deals, money. If it involved the Mob, not just the Outfit in Chicago, if any Mob needed assistance with nearly anything in Las Vegas, Johnny Roselli was the man to see. He worked for all the Mobs and all the owners. He orchestrated Hughes' arrival in Las Vegas, and the purchase of the Desert Inn, the Frontier, and many other Strip properties. And for each deal he put together, Johnny Roselli was given his piece of the action.

Bob Maheu called Roselli and asked him to get this damn problem with Howard Hughes solved. And Roselli did just that. He called Jimmy Hoffa at his home in Detroit, and he asked a favor.

Hoffa immediately called Ruby and told Ruby Kolod to "leave poor Howard alone for a while ... he likes it up there on the ninth floor." "Ruby...go tell Moe, it'd be a favor that I'm asking."

It worked. In the mid 1960s there was no one who had more power in Las Vegas than Moe Dalitz, but when Jimmy Hoffa calls and asks a favor . . . Anyway, it bought Hughes some time.

And then, so the story goes, Bob Maheu came up with an idea. Howard should just buy the place. Maheu explained to Hughes the two big plusses in buying the Desert Inn: (a) He wouldn't have to move out of the ninth floor, and (b) He wouldn't be taxed as heavily by Uncle Sam; the investment was active income.

"And, by the way, Howard," said Maheu, "gross revenue from a casino, 'gambling money,' is also considered active income. It'll be a wonderful tax advantage."

It wasn't only the Strip hotels that Hughes acquired. He became the largest landholder in Nevada. One of his purchases was 27,000 acres of cheaply bought desert on the outskirts of Las Vegas. What was called the "Husite Property" consisted of sand, cactus, and sagebrush. It was so far out and desolate, that the jackrabbits didn't even like the place.

But the 27,000 acre Husite Property now belonged to Howard Hughes.

And he bought up nearly all the gold and silver mines in the state. There were a lot of salty old prospectors who were deciding what they were going to do with all the money that this loony billionaire had given them for a mine which "hasn't been worth spit in 20 years."

What made Vegas even more attractive was that it had no personal or corporate income tax, nor inheritance, franchise, or warehouse taxes. The sales tax was only 3 percent, and real estate taxes were limited by the state constitution.

So, after a few months of haggling over the price, Howard Hughes bought the Desert Inn from Moe Dalitz and his partners. He paid a total of $13 million for the property. He left Dalitz and Ruby Kolod and most of the other managers at the DI in place and began his quest of collecting Las Vegas Strip hotels.

Howard's handlers, who were controlling many of his day-to-day decisions, had to bring in massive communication systems and all the other infrastructure systems that Hughes' Nevada Operations required. And not only his Nevada operations, but his worldwide operations. This never was a spur-of-the-moment decision. The owner of Hughes Tool Company and RKO Studios and TWA doesn't decide to take a little vacation in Las Vegas and then suddenly decide to stay on. The Hughes empire's move to Las Vegas had been planned for years.

Moe Dalitz and many other Las Vegas powerhouses knew that Hughes had a half billion that he needed to invest, and Las

Vegas might just be what he'd like to invest in.

Things were getting pretty hot for the casino owners in Las Vegas in 1966. There was some obvious skimming going on, and some Mobsters around town who had to be kicked out and made to understand that Las Vegas was for good, upstanding, tax-paying gamblers.

The hotels that Hughes added to his empire weren't picked out at random. You don't check "For Sale" signs hanging from Las Vegas hotel marquees. Most casino insiders understood that the Desert Inn, Sands, Castaways, Frontier, and the Silver Slipper all had two things in common:

1. Meyer Lansky was involved in all the hotels Hughes purchased, and,

2. Every one of the hotels that Hughes bought – every one of them – had an outstanding loan with the Central States Teamsters Pension Fund.

Before his monopoly game was over, Howard Hughes bought the Desert Inn, the Sands, Castaways, New Frontier, and the Silver Slipper on the Strip. He then bought Harold's Club in Reno.

The purchase of the Sands from Jack Entratter and Carl Cohen for $14.5 million is perhaps the most bothersome of all to me.

On the employee bulletin board of the Sands was hung a sign:

"Things are gonna change around here."

And did they ever. Jack Entratter, the single greatest entertainment director in the history of Las Vegas, at the Sands since 1952, currently president of the Sands, now had a new boss, Hughes' man, Howard Kane.

And Carl Cohen, the greatest casino boss in the history of the Strip, had to clear things through his new boss, Bob Maheu. And so it went down the line. Nothing over $10,000 could be spent without approval from Howard Hughes. The credit privileges which had kept the Sands rolling in money for years now required approval from upstairs. No longer could the pit bosses, who knew their customers, say yes or no to a credit request. The request had to be in writing, had to clear the accounting office and so on.

The services of call girls, which had been so commonplace at the Sands (along with all the other Strip hotels), were no longer available. Things were gonna be cleaned up under Mr. Hughes, and sure enough, the high rollers began to take up Caesars Palace on their offers and started staying over there.

The morale among the Sands employees dropped dramatically. Howard Hughes had an elaborate system of surveillance equipment installed in the casino, which included hidden cameras and daily computer printouts of "expected vs actual performance on a table game."

The computers were able to instantly spot a table where there appeared to be some irregularity in receipts. Dealers and casino employees were under constant surveillance by concealed electronic devices.

The dealers we used to know, and we used to like, because they were relaxed and enjoyed their jobs, and were encouraged to be nice and friendly, were gone. It was a whole new persona the dealers had to wear now. Even small talk was discouraged for the dealers. They could answer questions, but they were there to hit their "expected performance" level at the table, and casual conversation was a sure-fire way of slowing down the expected number of hands dealt per hour.

We weren't high rollers, but we were regulars. The Sands could count on us to lose our few hundred dollars per visit each and every time. The place changed. It wasn't the same after 1967. There was always a feeling of "business" about the place.

And one day, just before we were going to drive up to Las Vegas (we lived in LA at the time), my wife said to me, "Why don't we try the Riviera this time?" And we did, and we liked it. I'm sure there were thousands of other couples and hundreds of big-time gamblers who began doing the same thing. The Sands just wasn't the same any more.

Then, a couple of months after Howard Hughes moved into Las Vegas, there was the famous fight between Sinatra and Carl Cohen. Sinatra threw a chair, Cohen threw a right; the chair missed, the right didn't; and Sinatra walked out on his two remaining shows that night. Jack Entratter, still producing all the shows at the Sands, asked Alan King to come in and take over Sinatra's shows.

The Sands was a small hotel. Word of the fight spread around the hotel quickly, and within the hour everyone, employees as well as guests, was aware of what happened. Battle lines had been drawn between the new staff made up of Hughes' people, and the old Sands group, and there was a lot of tension in the air that permeated the entire operation.

Howard Hughes was the largest landholder in Nevada, owning more casinos than anyone else anywhere, yet he didn't do much for the state or the city. He didn't build any new hotels or even make any improvements on any of the hotels he bought.

He did a nice thing for his elderly grandmother, though. The Husite Property he had bought, the 27,000 acres of desert that the jackrabbits even thought was too far out, just before he left Las Vegas, he decided to rename that acreage after his grandmother, Amelia Summerlin.

THE GREAT STARDUST SKIM

1966

This is such a wonderful American success story. In 1976 the president of the Stardust Hotel was 34-year-old Allan Glick. Seemingly out of nowhere, this nice clean-cut young man and head of the Argent Corporation secured a Teamsters' loan for about $146 million that enabled him to take over the Stardust Hotel and Casino. (The Argent name was an abbreviation of **Allan R. Glick Ent**erprises.)

The timing on this loan was very important. By 1976, many of the Las Vegas casino "cash cows" the Mob depended on were beginning to dry up. Between the federal government and the state of Nevada, it was becoming more and more difficult for a Mobster to make a decent living. The Chicago Outfit still had control over the Stardust, Fremont, and Hacienda, but it became necessary to increase the size of the skim to make up for other lost business.

Let's take a moment to discuss the meaning of the word *skim*. It isn't stealing in the usual sense. It isn't taking money that belongs to someone else. Skimming is hiding money from Uncle Sam. Every time a dollar would come into the casino, it had to be reported to the government. So at the end of the year, when the Stardust would do its 1040-EZ or whichever form they used, they would have to pay income tax on every penny the casino took in.

How much more profitable would it be if the US government and Nevada state revenue people just didn't know how much money the Stardust and the other hotels had actually made? *("Wow! What a good idea! That way, we could get to keep a lot more of the money, right boss?")*

In the old days in Las Vegas this was easy to do. A casino owner could wander into the "soft count" room where the bills were counted, take a few handfuls of the big ones, put them in his pocket and then go have a cup of coffee and a Danish. Who was going to stop him? He owned the place. This was his money. He wasn't stealing. He just wanted to take a few thousand bucks as "walking around money." What Uncle Sam doesn't know ain't gonna' hurt him, right?

Then the hotel owner could find a nice corner on a hot-looking craps table, call Tony D., the pit boss there at craps pit 3, have Tony D. bring him a marker for "10 large," sign the marker, and get $10,000 in chips. He'd play a few minutes, lose a couple of thousand, scoop up the remaining 8 G's in chips, take them over to the cashier and cash out.

When his signed marker arrived in the accounting department, his girlfriend, Lola, would take the $10,000 marker and put it in her pocket. *("Honest, she's not my girlfriend, sweetheart, I hardly know the woman.")* And that was that. No marker means no money owed the casino, right? It's his money anyway, right? Who is he stealing from – himself?

Believe it or not, this very simple method of taking a few million dollars out of the Las Vegas hotels worked – year after year after year. Then the Nevada Tax and Gaming Commission boys set down some rules.

Rule Number 1 – An owner is never allowed in a counting room.

Rule Number 2 – An owner is never allowed to play at his own hotel.

Rule Number 3 – All money that comes into a casino – 100 percent of the money – has to be reported as income.

The US government trained its eyes on the casino business through the Organized Crime Commission, the Kefauver Committee, and, later, the Church Committee. Despite all the fed's money spent on all the investigations of the Las Vegas hotels and their owners, of all sorts of crimes, the only thing they could get the owners on was good old tax evasion.

Skimming money means taking money from the pot before Uncle Sam has a chance to count it and tell you how much tax you owe on it. If the money can't be counted, it can't be taxed – plain and simple.

There was a problem going on with the Recrion Corporation. Recrion owned, among other things, the Stardust Hotel. There was an early, and ongoing investigation, going on about skimmed money from the Stardust finding its way to Cleveland, Milwaukee, and Chicago. Moshe Rockman of Cleveland, Frank Balistieri of Milwaukee, and Joey Auippa of the Chicago Outfit were making a lot of money from the Recrion properties, and the stock in Recrion was the give-away.

The massive profits that Recrion was making was allowing insiders to profit from stock manipulation. Wild stock swings were not that unusual, and when the SEC began investigating, they found that corporate profits were going to buy stock, which was given to officers of the company.

Right up until June 19, 1975, Sam "Momo" Giancana had run Chicago. However, Momo wasn't the best of bosses of the Chicago Outfit. He was highly visible, having both a very flamboyant personality and a much publicized affair with singer Phyllis McGuire.

Then there was his friendship with Frank Sinatra. And with Judy Campbell, and with the Rat Pack. He was just too visible for the old school dons. And on top of everything else, their money stream, Las Vegas, was delivering less and less money. Enough was enough.

Late one night, in the basement kitchen of his Oak Park, Illinois, mansion, Sam made himself a before-bedtime snack of Italian sausage and peppers. He should have known better. That kind of food, especially right before bed, can kill you.

On the way to his bedroom, Sam was shot six times in the face. And Joey Auippa became *capo* of the Chicago Outfit.

No such thing as a "honeymoon period" for Joey Auippa either. The feds and the Nevada State Gaming Commission, who were both developing real power in Nevada, were beginning to make daily visits and phone calls to Auippa. It seems all they wanted to talk about was the Stardust. The question of real ownership of the Stardust, which had been hidden for many years, was beginning to bubble to the surface.

At the same time, Allan Glick, who had just turned 32, was beginning to make quite a few bucks at the Hacienda. He knew the Hacienda was a wonderful hotel and all, but it wasn't going to ever be a big-time casino. Talk about a fortuitous set of circumstances. Here were the owners of the Stardust being told to get out or lose their license, and here was Allan Glick, a nice, clean-cut young man who wanted desperately to get into the big time.

So Allan Glick spread the word all over Las Vegas that he wanted to buy the Stardust. His big problem was that he didn't have the money to buy it. But he let it be known, "If anyone wants to lend me the $100 million to buy it, I wouldn't say no."

One day, Glick got a phone call at his Hacienda office

from Del Coleman, the largest stockholder in the Recrion Corporation. Coleman, besides his Recrion affiliation, was also the unofficial representative of the Teamsters Union and the Chicago Outfit in Las Vegas. That meant he watched over their business affairs. Del Coleman said, "Allan, we got somebody you should meet," and Allan was introduced to the boss of the Milwaukee Mob, Frank Balistieri.

Balistieri said he could help Glick get a loan. A friend of his was an official at the Teamsters Central States Pension Fund. Then Glick started getting calls from some of the other Mob families, all wanting to be helpful to Glick in getting the Stardust loan. One call came from Kansas City. Glick was told the caller knew another Central States Teamsters official who could help arrange the loan. Then more calls came into Allan Glick's office from very well-connected and very friendly men from Cleveland, Cincinnati, and Chicago. And believe it or not, just like in the movies, the money started coming in.

Before long, our hero, Allan Glick, had enough money to buy the Recrion Corporation along with all of its assets including the giant Stardust Hotel. And all for next to no money out of his own pocket! Nearly $140 million was raised to install this nice young man as owner of the Recrion Corp. What a wonderful country we live in.

Al Sachs, who was president of the Stardust during the Recrion days, was the last to be replaced.

Allan Glick, president of Argent Corporation, just added Recrion Corporation and its assets to his holdings. The name Recrion disappeared and the Argent Corp was the owner of three hotels. He packed his bags and moved from the Hacienda to the president's suite at the Stardust. On his first day at his new job, Glick hired bookmaker-dealmaker-oddsmaker Frank "Lefty" Rosenthal to be his assistant at a salary of "250 large."

That same day, Lefty replaced Bobby Strella, who was a pretty good casino boss at the Stardust, with a fella whose previous job experience was owner-operator of the gift shop at Circus Circus, which he purchased for peanuts. The gift shop at Circus Circus was given as a favor to one of Momo Giancana's friends from Chicago at a "friends and family" price of $70,000. It was probably worth four times that much, but it was being sold to a Friend of Ours, *capice?*

When Tony Spilotro was at Circus Circus, he called himself Tony Stewart, but when he moved to the Stardust he went back to his original name. Spilotro was a hit man, a street-enforcer, and Mob killer who worked for the Chicago Outfit. He had been sent to Las Vegas a few years earlier by Sam Giancana to learn the city and to watch out for Chicago's interests there. The movie *Casino* starring Joe Pesci as the Tony Spilotro character and Robert De Niro as the Lefty Rosenthal character was one of the better Las Vegas Mob movies, in my opinion.

OK, Recrion was out as owners of the Stardust. They were bought out, not kicked out, and they were happy with their $30 million or so of profit. Sure, a few of them had to go to prison, but overall, it was a good ownership transition. However, there was a problem with Rosenthal's position as Stardust general manager. Lefty had a "past." He was a known associate of the Mob and had a conviction on his police record for fixing a basketball game some years earlier. Rosenthal's conviction, however, was conveniently removed from the record before he arrived in Las Vegas. But the guys who made up the Nevada Gaming Commission knew gambling and gamblers, and Lefty Rosenthal had a reputation which preceded him.

On the second day of Rosenthal's new job at the Stardust, the gaming authorities called Allan Glick and advised him that Lefty was never going to be given the "key employee" designation – ever. By the mid-1970s the Nevada Gaming Commission, commonly referred to as the NGC, said that every employee who worked in a key position within a casino that had a gaming license was going to be called a key employee. As a key employee, they, too, had to have a gaming license.

Allan Glick had to tell this news to Rosenthal. Glick was perfectly aware that Lefty was fully running the Stardust, even though he'd only been on the job for two days. Glick found Lefty and told him the news. What's in a title, right? Lefty gave up his position as general manager/casino manager and became the Stardust Hotel's poker room coordinator. As a lowly poker room coordinator, he wouldn't get that stupid key employee designation, and he didn't need a license.

He was still making his $250,000 and he still oversaw every single detail at the Stardust. Just to make it look even more presentable to the gaming guys, Rosenthal took over one of the poker tables as his permanent office. No one else sat there. It was in the back of the poker room with a phone on the table, and he worked there right in the open. The Nevada Gaming Commission then told him that he couldn't be the poker room coordinator, either. It seems the NGC had just made Las Vegas poker room coordinators key employees as well.

Not to be outdone, Lefty became the assistant entertainment director of the hotel for a while, and when those bureaucrats at the NGC said "no" to that, he became the assistant marketing manager. When that was stopped, he began broadcasting a nightly show from the Stardust interviewing celebrities on a Las Vegas television channel. This ploy of musical jobs really did work for quite a few years.

Lefty Rosenthal was running the Stardust Hotel, Tony Spilotro was taking care of the casino and any other problems that might arise, and Allan Glick was off playing golf down at La Costa on the California coast. Everyone seemed to be in place. Rosenthal had understood from day one what was expected of him. Chicago was deadly serious about making the Stardust and their other Las Vegas properties more profitable.

Two murders take place during this story, and the first one happens right about here. Marty Buccieri was a casino boss at Caesars Palace. Marty had been instrumental at the beginning of Allan Glick's money search by introducing Allan to some of his friends in Chicago.

One day Buccieri showed up at the Stardust looking for Allan Glick. Marty was told that Allan probably was down in the coffee shop, or maybe still in San Diego, or "you might want to try the health club." Buccieri found Glick in the steam room and told him that he owed him money – a finder's fee. He said something like: "I put you together with my boss, and look at you now. You own this joint. It was me who got you the $100 million and I want my piece. And I want it by next week."

Glick found Lefty Rosenthal, which wasn't all that hard to do. Lefty had taken over Glick's office in the executive suite. Glick told him about the meeting he just had in the Stardust health club with Marty and all the noise he was making. A week later, Buccieri was found sitting in the front seat of his car in the Caesars Palace parking lot. He had just left work, and someone was waiting in the back seat of his car, and popped him twice in the head with a 22-caliber pistol. A small-time Las Vegas hood named Horton was arrested for the murder. All Horton would ever say was that he shot Buccieri because he "wised off at me."

There were so many quarters and dollar tokens coming into the hard count room every night, it was physically impossible to count them with any accuracy. However, they could be weighed.

The casinos would purchase super-sensitive scales that could tell with nearly perfect accuracy how many quarters were being deposited at the end of a shift.

Frank " Lefty" Rosenthal

Keeping numbers simple: Say the Stardust weighed its quarters only once a day, at midnight. On this particular day, slot players had dropped 4,000 quarters into the various slot machines on the floor of the Stardust.

The slot machines would be emptied of their 4,000 quarters, the quarters would be put into some canvas bags, placed in those steel cages you see rolling around the casino, attended by visibly armed Stardust security guards. They roll those carts full of coins into the hard count room. (The soft count room is for counting bills.)

OK, 4,000 quarters is $1,000 and weighs exactly 10 pounds. So when the 10 pounds of quarters are put into the machine, the screen lights up $1,000. And the fellow who's watching over there, the guy with the clipboard in his hand, the one who's writing down $1,000, works for the Nevada Gaming Commission.

He has one job. He watches those screens, which show how much money all those quarters are worth. If the screen says $1,500 on the next weigh, he writes the $1,500 down just below the $1,000, and the last two weighs that the super-sensitive scale showed, meant that the Stardust had just shown that it had $2,500 that it had to account for.

It's here where the scheme begins –

Argent owned three hotels: the Stardust, Fremont, and the Hacienda. Each day the coins from the Fremont would be put into coin bags and taken by armored car to the Stardust. Coin bags from the Hacienda would also arrive at the Stardust by armored car. The bags would be opened and poured through chutes directly into hoppers located atop big scales. Argent hired a scale mechanic who recalibrated these scales perfectly so when 4,000 quarters ($1,000) were placed in the hopper, it only registered as $900. It was simple enough – $1,000 input and $900 output. *("All right, if it's working so well on the quarters, let's recalibrate those machines over there that weigh the dollar tokens.")*

The $900 in silver coins and dollar tokens was handled exactly by the book. Each roll was inspected and initialed by a Stardust employee as to accuracy. The tokens were recirculated onto the floor for resale and replay or were placed in the Stardust's bank account. But what do you do with the dollar coins and tokens? A few silver dollars can be passed at the grocery store to pay your bill, but not in great quantity. But try to spend $1 tokens from the Stardust that have the Stardust logo on them. There's not a lot of places anywhere except the Stardust that will take them from you. So what the heck are you going to do with all those tokens?

Back in 1975, in every casino in Las Vegas with the

exception of the Stardust, if you wanted change from the "change girls," they would sell it to you. Then they'd take your $20 bill, along with all the other bills, to the cashier's cage "employees only" window. They'd hand over the bills and get more rolls of coins in return. This was the standard way of dispensing coins in a casino.

The Stardust, however, told their change girls that instead of going to the cashier's cage, they were to go to a few locked coin cabinets placed against the walls around the casino. With a key to the cabinet, they'd take the bills and $1 tokens, put them in the drop box inside the cabinet, take the correct number of rolls, and get back to work. The change girls knew damn well that the "honor system" required them to take the correct number of rolls each time. They also knew the cameras were watching them. To try to swipe a roll of coins was absurd – and they all knew it.

What they didn't know was that this cabinet situation was the backbone of a multi-million-dollar skim, the largest casino skim ever uncovered in Las Vegas. And it involved only slot machines. Dozens of times a day, each change girl would open one of the coin cabinets with her key, deposit her money into the slot and take the right amount of wrapped coins. What they were taking was the 10 percent residue from the hard count room. Those coins that were not weighed by the ultra-sensitive scales, the $1 coins, were being turned back into foldable cash through this elegant little system of washing tons and tons of quarters and dollars. And there were literally tons of them. It was not unusual for one of these illegal coin boxes on the floor to have $10,000 in bills in it each evening when it was emptied.

Additionally, an "extra" change booth was set up on the Stardust floor. For quite a few years it was never noticed by the State – like a toll booth set up on a stretch of two-lane road in the dead of night. It looked and operated just like all the other change booths: get in line and change your bills into coins, get in line and change your coins into bills.

Except this change booth wasn't registered with any governmental authority. One hundred percent of the money that came in went directly to the coffers of Joey Auippa and the Chicago Outfit.

These coin cabinets around the casino and the extra change booth worked for nearly five years. It finally came out in the 1979 and 1980 trials that the quarter and dollar skim was so successful at the Argent properties that the Chicago Mob was receiving $15 million per year for each of five years.

As an aside to this story: There was a very sharp slot department manager working at the Fremont Hotel downtown. His name was Jay VanDermark. He was extremely valuable because he allegedly set up the entire skim operation there. All the little things necessary to take $300,000 per week out of the Argent properties were allegedly designed and implemented by VanDermark.

One of the first things Lefty Rosenthal did after he was brought in was to move VanDermark from the Fremont to the flagship of Argent Corporation, the giant Stardust.

VanDermark came in, managed the entire slot department, and watched over the day-to-day operation of the skim. As a special "thank you," Jay was given an all-expense paid trip to Mazatlan in Mexico. He was murdered while on the trip, the second murder in the story. All the loose ends were now tied up.

And this elegant little plan worked for the next four years.

THE SILVER SLIPPER'S SLIPPER

As you're driving on Las Vegas Boulevard South, you know that parking lot between the Stardust and the Frontier? That big empty lot that's really just an overflow lot for the Frontier? That used to be the home of the Last Frontier Village and the Silver Slipper Casino.

It was a nice old casino with a colorful history. Among the "firsts" at the Slipper: it was the first to hire female 21 dealers, the first place on the Strip where you could play poker, and it was the largest horse book on the West Coast.

Lots of great stories surround the horse book including some "past posting" incidents. The Slipper became a nice lowbrow joint with lots of Sands celebrities hanging out there – Sinatra, Sammy, and the real honcho at the Sands, Jack Entratter. It was a place they could let their hair down and get away with all kinds of things.

Shelby Williams from Texas bought the Slipper back in the mid 1960s, when it was kind of already slipping. It really couldn't compete with a lot of the "carpet joints" on the Strip – the real upscale hotels that were attracting more and more gamblers. Then one night, at the end of 1966, a fire started in a storage area.

It still, to this day, has never been proven to be anything but an "accidental fire of unknown origin," but it sure got Shelby Williams well again. His fire insurance premiums on the hotel were paid right up to date, fortunately.

No one was injured in the fire, but the Gaiety Theater, home of Minsky's Follies, had to be evacuated in mid-performance. The Minsky girls poured out of the showroom into the parking lot in high heels and big feather headdresses – and not much else! Eddie Cantor happened to be in the parking lot with his camera and took lots of photos of these beautiful showgirls standing around in next to nothing with the fire in the background. The pictures, by the way, are now in the possession of the Nevada Historical Society in Las Vegas.

Enter Howard Hughes.

There are so many great stories about Hughes, and many of them are true. This is probably one of them. Howard was, of course, a recluse. He lived on the penthouse floor of the Desert Inn, and his bedroom was directly across the street from guess what? The Silver Slipper's Slipper!

That's the Silver Slipper's slipper where Hughes believed the photographer was hidden, taking photos of Hughes in his bedroom.

That's the Slipper that twirled in the air and was the symbol of the Silver Slipper. It was big, 65 feet off the ground and hollow. One day Hughes, who was always protective of his privacy, decided a cameraman, either from the federal government or from the media, could hide inside that slipper. As the shoe twirled slowly, Hughes was sure he was being photographed in his own bedroom. He contacted Shelby Williams, the Silver Slipper owner (well, Hughes didn't contact Williams, it was Howard's man Bob Maheu who contacted

Shelby) to stop that "damn slipper from rotating."

Hughes insisted the hollowed out portion of the slipper be "filled in" so no one could sit inside it and take his picture. One never laughed at Hughes, but Williams came very close – and of course, turned down the request.

Within the week, Hughes owned the Silver Slipper (cost about $5.4 million). The Slipper in the air never turned again. It was filled in with concrete.

You can't be too careful, you know!

LEFTY AND THE ANT

Tony Spilotro was from Chicago. He was one of the lucky people who found his calling fairly early in life. He wanted to grow up to be a Mob enforcer – a very successful Mob enforcer.

He enjoyed violence and pain, especially if he was the one inflicting it.

Not long out of Steinmetz High School in Chicago, Tony first became an enforcer for "Mad Sam" DeStefano who had a reputation for torturing his victims. Tony fit in very well with the DeStefanos, catching the notice of the bosses in Chicago.

And with dedication and practice, Tony honed his enforcement skills. He was one of the truly scary people in the Chicago Outfit.

Back in the late 1950s through late 1970s, Las Vegas was a wonderfully successful business venture for the Mob. Tony "the Ant" worked for the Outfit. His boss, Tony Accardo, sent him to Las Vegas to watch out for Chicago's interests. Tony's expertise up to this point in his life had been the streets of Chicago.

Tony was the third of three fairly famous "Outside Men" that Chicago sent to Las Vegas.

Johnny Roselli was sent, in the late 1940s by Frank Nitti and Paul Ricca.

Marshall Caifano was sent to replace Roselli in 1950 by Sam Giancana.

Johnny Roselli was sent to replace Caifano in 1960 by Tony Accardo.

Marshall Caifano was sent to replace Johnny Roselli, again by Sam Giancana.

Sam Giancana was killed in his mansion at 1104 So. Winonah in Oak Park, 1975.

Tony Spilotro was sent to replace Caifano in 1971 by then boss, Joey Auippa.

Johnny Roselli was found in pieces in a 55-gallon drum floating off Miami, 1976.

Don Angelini was sent to replace Spilotro who was murdered in 1985.

OK, it gets a little complicated here, but this is how it played out: The Central States Pension Fund of the Teamsters Union – nearly $2 billion strong – the Fund, which Jimmy Hoffa's man, Allen Dorfman, would later be convicted of manipulating, loaned $43 million to Jay Sarno, so that Jay could open Circus Circus in 1968.

Spilotro was ready to make the move into Las Vegas. In 1970, Jay Sarno was still president of Circus Circus and got a call from Chicago. He was asked, probably by Joey Auippa, to sell the gift shop at the hotel to a "nice young man who we're sending out there. His name is Tony Stewart."

Jay met with Tony and told him that he'd sell him the rights to run the gift shop for $70,000. At the time, the gift shop, which wasn't doing that well, was worth in the neighborhood of $400,000. Sounded great, however, Tony didn't have $70,000.

Just like the big boys who borrowed millions of dollars from the Teamsters Central States Pension Fund, Tony decided that that was an avenue worth exploring for him, also. So he contacted Allen Dorfman, who was the man who had lent Jay Sarno the money to build Caesars and Circus Circus.

Dorfman said there was really no way that the giant Pension Fund could actually lend out an amount as small as $70,000 without raising all kinds of red flags.

However, Dorfman knew that Tony Stewart, as he was calling himself, had to get funding to get the gift shop going at Circus. This was going to be one of those loans that had to be made. Dorfman of course, knew who Tony Stewart really was.

So, this is how it was done: A company was set up in Deming, New Mexico, called the American Pail Corporation. American Pail had two officers, Irv Weiner of Niles, Illinois, and Donald DeAngeles of Port Richey, Florida.

The two owners of American Pail applied for a $1.4 million loan from the Central States Pension Fund. As the loan application was expected, Allen Dorfman had already approved the $1.4 million. Two other votes on the Teamster Fund board were required for the loan, and Jack Sheetz of Dallas and Al Matheson, a lawyer from Detroit who was also a Fund Trustee, approved the loan.

Allen Dorfman called Tony and told him that he'd have the $70,000 that he needed within 10 days. *"And thank you for using your Teamsters Central States Pension Fund."*

The $1.4 million check was made out to American Pail Company of Deming, New Mexico. And over dinner that night at Allen Dorfman's mansion in suburban Deerfield, the $1.4 million was split up.

Irwin Weiner and Don DeAngeles, the two guys who set up and co-owned American Pail down in New Mexico, were given their cut of the proceeds. Tony Stewart was given the $70,000 that he needed, plus some extra money, just for good luck when he opened the gift shop, and after some minor expenses, such as thank you gifts to Jack Sheetz of Dallas, Al Matheson of Detroit, and the pension fund trustees who OK'd the loan, the bulk of the loan went into the bank account of Allen Dorfman.

And Tony Stewart, whose real name was, of course, Tony Spilotro, got his $70,000 bankroll, paid it to Jay Sarno and opened up the Circus Circus gift shop. Anthony Stewart, Ltd., was the name of his shop.

As planned all along, the Circus Circus gift shop was Tony's headquarters for his loansharking and bookie operations. Before Tony came to Las Vegas, the biggest loanshark and bookie in town was over at the Leaning Tower of Pizza.

But it didn't take Tony long to corner the market on people who wanted to bet using illegal bookies. With legitimate bookies available everywhere in Las Vegas, why would anyone want to go to an illegal bookie? Because if you walk into Caesars to make a bet, the person behind the counter isn't going to give you your ticket unless you give him your money first.

By using one of the illegal bookies in town, you didn't have to worry about paying, if at all, until Wednesday. That's a valuable service to a large betting population.

The liability for the bookie or the loan shark is that sometimes the people who bet with an illegal bookie don't have the cash on them today, but they're expecting a big check on Saturday. Tony had a couple of real good collection people who looked forward to coming to work each day.

It didn't take long for word to get out that Tony Stewart and Tony Spilotro were the same person.

As soon as the Nevada Gambling Commission became aware of Spilotro's presence in Las Vegas, they exerted as much pressure on Jay Sarno as they could to get Sarno to throw Spilotro the hell out of Circus Circus, and the hell out of Las Vegas!

Very few people wanted to go up against Tony Spilotro. The man had just the right qualifications to be Chicago's man in Las Vegas. He was absolutely ruthless, and he enjoyed killing people. And Sarno and nearly everyone else in the casino business in Las Vegas knew it. You don't mess with Tony Spilotro. And you certainly don't tell him to get the hell out of *his store*, and not come back anymore! I mean, that's just insanity. Let the NGC come in and tell Spilotro that he has to leave.

It wasn't until 1972, when Jay Sarno and his partners were bought out by the two Bills (Bill Pennington and Bill Bennett) that they were able to get Spilotro the hell out of Circus Circus. With the two Bills coming in, Tony knew that his gift shop days were over.

Pennington and Bennett told all the concession holders that the holding company for the casino hotel, Circus Circus Enterprises, would now be running all their own concessions. Pennington and Bennett called the NGC and told them that Spilotro was on his way out, "thank goodness."

So Tony Stewart had to find another place to office. But first, he had to sell the damn shop. He had paid $70,000 for it and sold it for $700,000.

William F. Roemer, Jr., in his book *The Enforcer* tells of how the buyers of the gift shop, the ones who agreed to the $700,000, had second thoughts the next morning. They decided that it wasn't worth that much, and they wanted to renegotiate the purchase price. Tony went over there and demanded the full amount, and the group immediately caved.

They had read about the "gift shop operator" in the *Las Vegas Review Journal* and the *Las Vegas Sun*, and the group decided that they "didn't want any trouble with that guy." Smart decision.

Sid Wyman and Morris Shenker

The boss of the Dunes for years had been Sid Wyman, and it was a good place to work. Then Sid died, and Morris Shenker took over.

Shenker was an attorney from Detroit, and like Tom Hagen in *The Godfather*, he had only one client. Hagen's client was Vito Corleone. Shenker's was Jimmy Hoffa. Morris Shenker spoke for Jimmy Hoffa.

Sid Wyman has been a real big-time poker player. And he loved playing in the Dunes card room. Everyone loved having him around, too, even if he was the boss.

Always a hello to everyone, usually by name. So what if they wore name tags, Sid was just that kind of guy.

When the Nevada Gaming Commission came down with the new rules for casino owners, one of them was that neither Sid Wyman, nor any other owner, was allowed to play in their own casino. Wyman used to love that poker room. It wasn't that he was just a good player, which he was, it was the size of his bets. He really loved no limit poker games.

When Sid died, all action in the Dunes was stopped for two minutes coinciding with the start of his funeral.

Anyway, Shenker came in, and the Dunes shuddered. He wouldn't spend a penny on the care and upkeep of the property, and, guess what, it went downhill, fast. But that wasn't all.

Starting in the early 1960s, until Morris Shenker came in, there was a guy named Big Julie, who worked out of New York, was one of the Dunes vice presidents. He was in charge of the junkets. He regularly chartered TWA planes and crews and brought high rollers in every week from New York, Miami, and St. Louis, and was pretty successful with it. No one did junkets better than the Dunes – but no more.

When Spilotro got his check for $700,000 for the sale of Anthony Stewart, Ltd., at Circus Circus, he headed over to the Dunes.

Shenker knew he was coming and set up a nice office for Spilotro, right in the back of the Dunes card room. Off by himself, at a big card table with his phone sat Tony Spilotro. Day after day, this was where Tony had his office, in the card room that Sid Wyman used to love.

Everyone who knew what was going on knew who Spilotro was, and that he was conducting business right out in the open at the Dunes. Spilotro wasn't a fun guy to be around, either. With Morris Shenker and Tony Spilotro there every day, and loss of all the benefits that the Dunes employees used to have under Wyman's rule, and hardly anyone smiling anymore, lots of Dunes employees began looking for something better. Nearly anything would do!

Lefty Rosenthal

At the same time, Argent Corp. was able to purchase Recrion Corp., which owned the Stardust. Allan Glick, president of Argent, put Tony and Lefty Rosenthal in charge of the hotel and casino.

Lefty Rosenthal was one of the all-time money men – a guy who was a genius with numbers, who could run the cash flow in and out of a major casino, even with the NGC watching, and the only problem Lefty's bosses were having was that they had to figure out where to hide that kind of hard cash on a weekly basis! (This wasn't electronic money – this was folded, older, and mixed bills.)

Lefty was keeping everyone happy with the profits he was delivering to Chicago. Tony was keeping things running smoothly, getting rid of any problems or potential problems or troublemakers or people he just didn't like.

Then one day, Tony's brother, Michael, who owned a pretty successful retail jewelry store in Las Vegas, began turning the Gold Rush, Ltd., from "pretty successful" into "wildly successful."

He began getting more and more jewelry, high grade stuff, and his acquisition costs were close to zero.

At the same time, lots of jewelry was being reported missing from all sorts of upscale homes in the guarded, gated communities off the Strip. The thieves would gain entry by cutting holes in the walls of these homes – hence, the name, "The Hole in the Wall Gang." Tony Spilotro and his brother, Michael, were running a ring of eight really top-notch jewel thieves.

The Hole in the Wall Gang was scoring big and bringing the loot to the Gold Rush, Ltd., where it was disposed of. Gold

Rush Ltd., was doing so well in selling hot merchandise that for quite a few years in the early 1970s, it was the best place on the West Coast to fence stolen merchandise. Michael ran the Gold Rush along with Tony's bodyguard, Fat Herbie Blitzstein. Blitzstein came out to Las Vegas from Chicago too. All 320 pounds of him. He was Tony's collector as well as bodyguard. Tony was a very small man, Fat Herbie Blitzstein was 6 feet 6 inches – but no one laughed when they saw the two of them walking together.

Michael and his big brother, Tony, were, according to court records, making "millions of dollars" yearly. Lefty Rosenthal was suspected of involvement, but was never charged – apparently the LVPD and the feds were eventually satisfied he was never involved in this "side business."

Las Vegas' current mayor, Oscar Goodman, was one of the most famous criminal defense lawyers in the country. His client list included some very high-profile Mobsters, including Tony Spilotro.

He's been in office since June 1999 and was elected to his second four-year term in 2003. Whenever you see Goodman on TV, the guy seems to be really enjoying himself. He calls himself the "Happiest Mayor in America."

He's been responsible for a lot of the revitalization of downtown, and most Las Vegans agree he's doing a pretty good job in office. In the 2003 election, Goodman was re-elected by a landslide – he received 86 percent of the vote!

At the same time, the profits from the Stardust began slipping – whether it was due to competition, or due to Tony's distractions caused by running this gang of jewel thieves, didn't matter.

He was making all kinds of money which didn't have to be shared with the bosses in Chicago. However, Chicago found out about the burglary ring within a few months.

The second week of June 1986, Tony and brother, Michael, were asked to "come into the office" in Chicago.

The last time the two brothers were seen alive was early in the evening of June 16th, leaving Tony's home in Oak Park.

Both the brothers had just been acquitted in a Chicago court after being charged with the "Hole in the Wall" burglaries. They thought this was going to be a celebration of their acquittal.

They were taken for a ride to an Indiana cornfield, beaten, and, according to autopsy results and superwriter Nick Pileggi, they were buried alive. Pileggi writes wonderful Mob stories. If this story seems familiar, you probably saw the movie he wrote, *Casino*. Spilotro in real life became Mickey Santoro in the movie. The Stardust was called the Tangiers. And Joe Pesci did a fabulous job portraying Tony. An excellent movie!

Because Lefty Rosenthal couldn't get a Nevada gaming license, he couldn't hold a key position at the Stardust any longer. He was made "beverage manager" of the hotel, and continued running day-to-day casino operations under that title.

The NGC said, no, he couldn't be a hotel employee at all. So he began hosting a TV show out of the Stardust – the *Lefty Rosenthal Show*. It was a late-night interview show, which was mildly successful, not because Lefty was a great interviewer, or host – he really wasn't, but he had lots of friends in Las Vegas who came on to "chat." Sinatra, for example, was a regular guest. If I remember correctly, the show aired at 1 a.m. – a logical time in Las Vegas for a TV show.

In October 1982, Lefty stopped for dinner at the Tony Roma's out on West Sahara. He came out, started his car, and it blew up. The bomb had been placed under a metal plate, however, which deflected the force of the bomb away from Lefty.

Lefty Rosenthal left Las Vegas and retired to South Florida. Most casino people would agree that Lefty Rosenthal was one of the greatest oddsmakers who ever lived.

COFFEE SHOP STORIES:
RAT PACK AND THE SANDS

There was no question – the Sands had to close. Even regulars, like my wife and me, began staying at the other hotels in the early 1980s. We still had the warm fuzzies for the Sands, and each trip out to Las Vegas we'd take a cab over, play a few hands of blackjack, and wander over to the Garden Terrace Coffee Shop for something to eat. After we were seated, and we usually wanted a table waaaaay in the back … reminiscent of the 1960s and 1970s when we took a back table after midnight, and with coffee and our 99-cent steak and eggs, we could watch the best floor show in Las Vegas.

They liked the back tables, too. Showgirls, well-known comedians, guys who you knew just had to be in the Mob, lots of Hollywood types, and the occasional superstar. We saw Jack Benny there a couple of times. He would come over after his set down at the Riviera and sit at a table near us.

I remember a table there in possibly 1964 or 1965 when Jan Murray, Jerry Lewis, Buddy Hackett, and Imogene Coca, plus two or three others we didn't recognize were sitting nearby, and they were all eating the 99-cent special too, and talking just like real people! Well, Jerry Lewis wasn't eating the 99-cent special. He ordered oatmeal and a bagel. The oatmeal was too cold or the bagel was too hard or the butter wasn't room temperature, we didn't know what the hell happened to upset him, but he really let the waitress have it. He was angry with her, and whatever it was that caused his wrath, it had to do with his food.

The waitress wasn't a kid, and I'm sure she had years of experience dealing with situations. Working in a coffee shop of a Strip casino, the chances are there isn't too much the waitress hadn't seen, or hadn't had to deal with, including an unbelievably rude Jerry Lewis.

The waitress took back his offending oatmeal, and even

while she was gone, he was talking about what a stupid woman ... *doesn't she know I like my oatmeal with ...* whatever, I don't even remember the cause of the problem. But my wife and I were sitting maybe 10 feet away from this. Jerry was loud, and everyone in the restaurant was aware of the fact that he was yelling at this nice elderly waitress, who was earning $1.20 an hour.

We saw Buddy Hackett many times at the Sahara and a few times at the fabulous coffee shop – The Garden Room. He was VP of Entertainment at the Sahara, with points in the hotel, and for years he was there exclusively. Anyway, Hackett was the very funniest person I'd ever seen in Las Vegas. And we saw him often, maybe three or four times a year. My wife and I were living in LA, and if Buddy Hackett was playing the Sands or the Sahara, we'd try to get up even for one night to catch his show.

If you're old enough to have seen Hackett back in the 1960s and 1970s, you know what he could do to an audience. Buddy Hackett was so funny that every time we saw his show, we'd also see people sitting on the floor laughing. I'd never realized that an adult could actually fall off a chair from laughing too hard.

My dad and I were at the Sahara and went to see Buddy Hackett in the Congo Room. At a booth right next to us, sitting in what was called "The Sinatra Booth" was Sinatra with two men I didn't recognize. One had to be his bodyguard, maybe they both were. In Las Vegas, Sinatra was never without a bodyguard. In the 1980s he had four bodyguards with him wherever he went. The Sinatra Booth was booth 1A, front and center, 15 feet back from the stage.

So Buddy Hackett comes out. Now we'd seen Hackett maybe 25 times, and he has eight or 10 different sets. We've heard all his routines, but each time you hear them they seem to be funnier and funnier. My dad and I were sitting at one of the smaller "B" tables, the lights go down, the music comes up a little, and from the wings: "Ladies and gentlemen, the Sahara Hotel is proud to present … Mr. Buddy Hackett!"

And Hackett walked out on stage naked. Not completely naked, he was wearing high-shine dress shoes and black socks. And that was it. Two shoes, two socks, and a microphone. He just stood there, with that wonderfully expressive face of his, in all his glory, not behind a podium, just standing in the middle of the stage with not the slightest reference to the fact that he's naked.

People who went to see Buddy Hackett were prepared for some of the things he did. He had a very "adult" show. He was one of the few stand-ups that children under 18 were not allowed in to see.

Now, here's the picture. Buddy Hackett naked with black socks and shoes. And most of the audience gasping for air. Frank Sinatra was howling. He was down on his hands and knees on the carpet in front of his booth, screaming in laughter. As was everyone else in the Congo Room.

The waiters – who've seen everything – were falling over with laughter. You knew that Hackett was going to be funny, that's why you came in. But walking out naked, and he'd now been up there like that for two or three minutes – it absolutely murdered the room. I saw a woman crawl past our table trying to get to the exit, but she was laughing too hard to make much progress.

Sinatra was sitting on the floor, with his back up against the booth, slamming his hands on the carpeting, telling Hackett to stop it, "Enough, you're killing me." It had to be five solid minutes – with Hackett fueling the laughter even more with his wonderful facial expressions.

We saw Lucy out by the pool, and later that weekend we rode down in the same elevator as Doris Day.

We remember sitting in the Garden Cafe, watching Harry Belafonte have breakfast. We saw Vice President Spiro Agnew and Nancy Sinatra and Bernadette Peters and Jimmy Connors and Groucho Marx (actually that encounter we could have done without).

We loved Groucho Marx, and we saw him in probably his last venture to Las Vegas, subdued and bent over, being pushed in his wheelchair by his nurse – the one he left the bulk of his estate to. Sure, we all get old, but I would have preferred to remember Groucho as he'd been 25 years earlier.

The Sands, along with most of the other resort hotels on the Strip, was "Mobbed up" during the Rat Pack years.

In the early 1960s, when Sinatra and the Rat Pack were playing the Sands, the owners of record, their percentage of ownership, and home addresses were as follows:

Hyman Abrams, 607 Boulevard, Revere, Mass., 9% ownership

L. R. Brooks, 407 Lincoln Road, Miami, Fla., 4%

Bryant Burton, 611 Wilshire Blvd., Los Angeles, Calif., 1%

Carl Cohen, Sands Hotel, Las Vegas, Nev., 9.5%

Jack Entratter, 720 E. Charleston Blvd., Las Vegas, Nev., 12%

Sadie Freedman (widow of Jake Freedman), Sands Hotel, Las Vegas, Nev., 12%

Harry Goldman, Albert Parvin & Co., 120 No. Robertson, Los Angeles, Calif., 2%

Charles Kendel, Sands Hotel, Las Vegas, Nev., 3%

Edward Levy, 804 So. Eighth Pl., Las Vegas, Nev., 4%

Dean Martin, 601 Mountain Dr., Beverly Hills, Calif., 1%

Albert Parvin, Albert Parvin & Co., 120 No. Robertson, Los Angeles, Calif., 2%

Maxwell Rubin, Albert Parvin & Co., 120 No. Robertson, Los Angeles, Calif., 2%

George Reese, Sands Hotel, Las Vegas, Nev., 1%

Jerry Ross, 608 No. Rexford Dr., Beverly Hills, Calif., 2.5%

Michael Shapiro, 1253 Camden Dr., Beverly Hills, Calif., 9%

Aaron Weisburg, Diplomat Apts., Paradise Road, Las Vegas, Nev., 4.5%

Treasury: 21% ("Treasury" refers to unassigned points in the Sands)

Later, Frank Sinatra would own 9 percent of the Sands from these treasury points. (His 9 percent of the Sands was valued at $380,000 for tax purposes.)

Some of the names of Sands owners not appearing on the Nevada Gaming Commission's "Licensees of the Sands Hotel and Casino" were:

Doc Stacher

Joey Fusco

Longy Zwillman

Tony Accardo

Sam Giancana

Al Teitelbaum (Mob lawyer)

Gerardo Catena (New Jersey Mob boss)

Johnny Roselli (representing the Chicago Outfit)

Joey Adonis

Frank Costello . . . and a few more

The Rat Pack Show

To get into the Sands show in the Copa Room when the Rat Pack was playing was very difficult. It was far and away the hardest ticket in Las Vegas to get. Jack Entratter, who ran the entertainment at the Sands, was the man who controlled who got tickets, and who didn't.

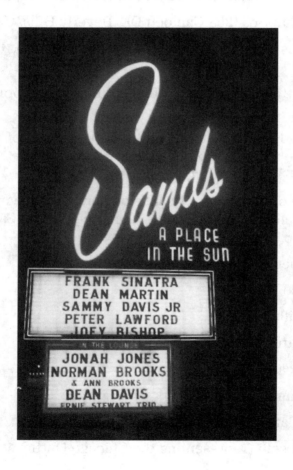

The Copa Room was a tiny showroom by today's standards. Ten years later, if you had the money to get in to see a "sold-out" Elvis show at the International or the Hilton, you could always find a ticket for sale. The MGM Theater had seating for 3,000 people. But when there are only 300 seats available, it's a completely different matter.

After the first performance, Jan. 20, 1960, the press really picked up on the Rat Pack. It was a fun show to attend. Casual, irreverent, it became popular in the press, and people from all over the country were reading about these five stars at the Sands. It seemed all the movie stars and big money people in Hollywood were going to the Sands when Sinatra and Deano and Sammy were there.

My wife and I saw the Rat Pack once. Long story short – one of the bellhops who'd been there since the Sands opened – either liked me or thought I was very funny. I was in the lobby of the Sands, waving around a $5 bill saying, "Looking for a ticket for the Sinatra show tonight." He laughed and said, "I'll get you into the show."

I told him I really couldn't thank him appropriately, we were pretty broke. He said, don't worry about it – asked my name, then said, "Oh, of course, Mr. F, I knew I recognized you" (they were so damn classy there). Sure enough, when we got on line for the midnight show, our names were on the reservation list.

We couldn't afford to tip the maitre d' – so we sat in the back – at one of those long tables with 16 people who you don't know. But we got in early, so we got to sit near the front of the table, facing one another, closest to the stage.

Behind us, in the very rear of the Copa Room, were the men with no names, the real power in the room. The guys who would wait until the show started, nod to the maitre d', and watch the show and the crowd from the back.

These were the owners – these men were connected. In the very front of the room, there was always the table with the three blondes – the girls with no last names, friends of Frank or Dean, and then the real big hitters and the name celebrities throughout the rest of the room.

Back when the Mob ran Vegas, there was a wonderful custom in the "big rooms." The celebrities in the audience would be introduced. They'd stand up, wave to the rest of us, and sit down.

The night my wife and I got in to see the Rat Pack, I remember Rosalind Russell being introduced, and Gregory Peck, and Bob Hope, and one or two more celebrities, and then Lucille Ball and Desi Arnez were pointed out. This was real big time.

In every showroom in Las Vegas, there are certain inviolate rules: Rule Number One is that the headliners go for 60 minutes. Not 58 minutes, not 59 minutes and certainly not 64 minutes. Those extra four minutes represented four minutes of lost revenue on the casino floor.

Deano came out on stage with his signature, *"Who are all you people – and what are you doing in my room?"* and so started the two and a half hours of the Rat Pack show.

After going to Las Vegas for over 40 years, and seeing nearly everyone who's played the big rooms there, you get kind of jaded, I guess. But we'd never seen anything like that night back in 1961, when we saw Frank Sinatra, Dean Martin, Sammy Davis, Jr., Joey Bishop, and Peter Lawford do their thing.

It seemed as if they were ad-libbing the entire time. Of course they weren't. Joey Bishop wrote most of the so-called ad-libbing for the show, and it was a well-rehearsed and smooth performance. It was magic. Funny, great dancing and imitations, and humor and Sinatra, when he sang, no one joked. He was never interrupted. In 1961 there wasn't a better voice anywhere. He had the room in absolute total silence. Everyone was mesmerized by The Voice.

And then Sammy came on. The entire room just couldn't get enough of these guys. This was a very hip audience – people were cheering at the end of every song, every changeover, we also stood up and cheered them at the very top of our voices.

For the first and only time in my life, I stood on a chair to cheer!

The Free Sands Coffee Mugs

After we'd leave the coffee shop, we'd stop over at that booth across from the gift shop – the one that gave away those Sands coffee mugs. *Just Present Your Out-of-State Drivers License.* Like everyone else who visited Vegas frequently, we still must have a mismatched set of 15 or so mugs around the house.

We once stayed on the top floor in one of those suites with two balconies – not that we paid for it, and certainly not because we were comped for it. Neither of us were, or are, big bettors, but it was just one of those lucky things. The fellow at the front desk had been there a lot of years, and he gave us the impression that he remembered us.

Whether that was the case, or maybe all the rooms that they had left in the Tower were high roller suites doesn't really matter, but we were given a fabulous one-bedroom and attached living room suite; it was probably a mini-suite, but the damn thing was two stories high – all glass wall and two wonderful balconies.

You know how you, me, and everyone else who goes to Las Vegas justifies staying in an inexpensive room, right? "Well, we don't spend much time in the room anyway." How many times have you heard that? For that three- or four-day stay, we spent an amazing amount of time in our room. The place was a palace. We even had room service meals out on one of the patios, overlooking the Strip. Just another one of our Sands memories.

On one of our trips in the late 1960s, my wife was given two black chips as a bribe to give up her seat at a really hot blackjack table. She was at a $2 table that was on fire. And she was the only bettor on the table who still had silver and a couple of red chips out on each bet. Everyone else was high-fiving and whooping it up – and betting stacks of blacks. Lots of noise, lots of cheering. The BJ table sounded like a good craps table. Ed Walters was shift manager at the time, and he was watching the table, as was the pit boss, a fellow named Tony. During the mid-1960s most of the pit bosses at the Sands were named Tony.

Anyway, a silk-suit with a big pinkie ring leans over my wife and hands her the two black chips, in exchange for her seat at the table. I didn't hear what he said, but afterward my wife told me that he was very courteous, and $200 is $200!

She also remembers that when he took her chair, Carl Cohen, who was casino manager, came over and said, "Hello, Mr. N – how're ya doin?" I looked over at the guy as we were leaving, and he was signing a marker. Mr. N bought my wife's blackjack table seat 40 years ago, and we've often wondered who he was.

Sammy Davis, Jr.

We had seen Sammy perform five different times, all in Las Vegas. Once was with the Rat Pack at the Sands, once with Bill Cosby at the Las Vegas Hilton, and three times we'd seen him do his solo act.

Of all the performers we've seen in Las Vegas over the years, Sammy still stands out as the most talented and totally enjoyable. But the most memorable occasion was seeing Sammy Davis, Jr., in person. We had an absolutely wonderful experience with this man, and I'm going to share it.

At home - at

The Sands HOTEL

Sammy Davis, Jr.

When the Sands was first built, it was a low-slung main building, housing the casino, restaurants, the Copa Room and so on. The hotel rooms were all in the back, garden-style two-story complexes, all named after famous race courses: The Belmont, Churchill Downs, Aqueduct, Santa Anita and so on. There were two pools at the Sands: the one that was right outside the fabulous Coffee Shop (The Garden Room) was called the Paradise Pool, and the smaller pool in the back was the Aqueduct Pool.

We preferred the Aqueduct Pool. It was out of the way, it was quieter, and the Rockingham Annex or the Hialeah Annex were both far less expensive to stay in than was the Tower – the main building.

There were three hidden areas at the Sands – probably a lot more than that – but three that I was aware of.

First, there was a hidden compound, a stand-alone apartment tucked away in the back between the Rockingham and the Aqueduct Annexes. That was Jack Entratter's apartment. Entratter was probably the reason the Sands was so popular for so many years. Jack was one of the owners of the hotel and was also the best entertainment director on the Strip.

When Howard Hughes bought the Sands in 1967, he purchased it from Jack Entratter and Carl Cohen.

There was another, nearly identical compound on the other side of the Aqueduct, next to the Hialeah. That was Frank Sinatra's. Frank used this apartment and office for some years.

Much later, after a long break from the Sands, he returned to star there and moved into the hotel with his own three-bedroom suite, first on the ground floor and then a three-bedroom, three-balcony suite on the 14th floor.

The third hidden enclave was a trailer. Way in the back of the Sands property, behind Sinatra's compound (it was very hidden). Unless you knew what it was, you'd walk right past it.

Back there were the six tennis courts – and right next to the tennis court was this trailer. It had its own parking places – entrance in the back – so you couldn't see comings and goings from the tennis court area. This was where Sammy Davis, Jr., lived when he entertained at the Sands.

For many years, all the way through the early 1960s, black entertainers were not allowed to stay in the Strip or the downtown hotels. A shame, but a fact of life through 1961 or 1962. It was Frank Sinatra who forced the issue at the Sands: "Sammy stays in the hotel, or I walk."

Anyway, one day my wife and I were playing tennis – and Sammy Davis, Jr., pulls into his parking space, gets out of his car, and picks up a ball that one of us knocked over the fence. He walks the tennis ball up to us, throws it over and starts visiting. What a total surprise. What a genuinely nice guy. Just conversation. He asked how we were doing on the tables, told us about a dinner he'd had last night at the House of Lords (at the Sahara). How he thought it was way overpriced, and not that great.

He told us that he was still experiencing a sore throat (what he called "Vegas throat") – long story here, too – but a lot of entertainers, especially singers, get it.

We told him we loved him on stage, he asked where we'd seen him – just a really pleasant 10- or 15-minute conversation with Sammy Davis, Jr. Something both my wife and I remember vividly to this day. What a nice, nice thing for him to do. Just thought I'd share that remembrance here. Of all the entertainers we'd seen over the years, Sammy is one that we miss most.

The Last Bet

Did you know the very last bet placed at the Sands was placed by Bob Stupak? He was given the honor of the last bet. I understand it was a $1,000 bet on the pass line. And I don't know if he won or lost. Nor have I ever found out why he was given that honor.

There was the downside to the closing, of course. It was the 1,500 Sands employees who were put out of work. From the time the Sands closed until the Venetian opened, you still have to feed your family. Lots of the Sands employees were old timers who'd been there for many years and were in their 50s and 60s. Hard to get a new job at that age.

Sheldon Adelson did set up a temporary hiring office and supplied job counseling and training right on site, but there were still 1,500 families who were hurt when the Sands closed. Including a good friend of ours. Even though we never saw him off the Sands property, and never saw him off his working hours, my wife and I used to joke about it. His name tag said, "Bill, New York." We'd always laugh and said his name tag should have read, "Bill, Bad Toupee." It was a really bad toupee, it didn't even match the color of his own hair peeking out.

He laughed about the hair mismatch more than the guests did. He was one of the nicest and funniest and most colorful blackjack dealers I've ever met. He was one of those employees who survived six different management changes at the Sands and had to retire five years before he wanted to. He told us that on our last visit there.

The Sands closed just before the July 4th weekend of 1996. You couldn't book a room for May or June 1996. Over 100 percent occupancy. Lots and lots of old timers wanted to stay there one more time. We went up in June of 1996, couldn't get into the Sands and ended up staying at the Flamingo. We got a good deal on our room, too. It was only $29 per night. Yes, it was overlooking the alley in the back, but how much time do you actually spend in your room anyway?

REFERENCES

Ainlay, Taj, Jr., and Judy Dixon Gabaldon. *Las Vegas - The Fabulous First Century*. Charleston: Arcadia Publishing, 2003.

"Alleged Illegal Bookmakers Tied to Buffalo Mob." *Las Vegas Review Journal*. June 16, 1991.

Basten Fred E. and Charles Phoenix. *Fabulous Las Vegas in the 50s*. Santa Monica: Angel City Press, 1995.

"Black Book Adds Perry 'the fixer'." *Las Vegas Review Journal*. Oct. 29, 1992.

Brill, Steven. *The Teamster*. New York. Simon and Schuster, 1979.

Cohen, Michael, *Mickey Cohen, In My Own Words*. London: Prentice Hall International, 1975.

Dahlberg, Tim. "State Says Argent Execs Allow Slot Machine Scam." *Las Vegas Review Journal*. May 31, 1979.

"Defer Action on Licenses for Hotels." *Las Vegas Review Journal*. March 15, 1955.

DeMatteo, Deanna. Las Vegas Strip History. http://www.lvstriphistory.com.

Denton, Sally and Roger Morris. *The Money and the Power*. New York: Alfred A. Knopf, 2001.

Edmonds, Andy. *Bugsy's Baby*. New York: Birch Lane Press, 1993.

Farrell, Ronald A. and Carole Case. *The Black Book and the Mob*. Madison: University of Wisconsin Press, 1995.

"Foil Hood Trying to Take Over Riviera Hotel." *Las Vegas Review Journal*. April 6, 1955.

Gibson, Elizabeth. *It Happened In Nevada*. Helena: Falcon, 2001.

Goldman, Albert. *Elvis*. New York: McGraw-Hill, 1981.

Goodman, Michael J. "Spilotro Moves Up and Around in Vegas." *Las Vegas Review Journal.* Feb 27, 1983.

"Gus Greenbaum, Mate Dead in Phoenix." *Las Vegas Review Journal.* Dec. 3, 1958.

Hopkins, A.D. and K. J. Evans. *The First 100 – Portraits of the Men and Women Who Shaped Las Vegas.* Las Vegas: Huntington Press, 1999.

"Hotel Riviera Slates Opening Next April 8." *Las Vegas Review Journal.* Dec. 22. 1954.

"Imprisoned Slot Cheat Placed in Nevada's Black Book." *Las Vegas Review Journal.* Feb 28, 1991.

Jennings, Dean. *We Only Kill Each Other.* New York: Pocket Books, 1967.

Kelly, Kitty. *His Way – Unauthorized Biography of Frank Sinatra.* New York: Bantam Books, 1986.

Lacey, Robert. *Little Man – Meyer Lansky and the Gangster Life.* Boston: Little, Brown and Company, 1991.

Las Vegas Review Journal. *Las Vegas – Through the Generations.* Marceline: D-Books Publishing, 1995.

Lawford, Patricia Seaton. *The Peter Lawford Story.* New York: Carrol and Graf Publishers, 1988.

Lebo, Harlan. *The Godfather Legacy.* New York: Fireside, 1997.

Levy, Shawn. *Rat Pack Confidential.* New York: Broadway Books, 1998.

Moore, Boyd. *Nevadans and Nevada.* San Francisco: H.S. Crocker, Inc. 1950.

Neff James, *Mobbed Up.* New York: Atlantic Monthly Press, 1989.

Newton, Wayne. *Once Before I Go.* New York: Avon Publishing, 1951.

Odessky, Dick. *Fly on the Wall*. Las Vegas: Huntington Press, 1999.

Ralli, Paul. *Nevada Lawyer*. Culver City: Murray and Gee, Inc, 1949.

Rappleye, Charles and Ed Becker. *All American Mafioso*. New York: Doubleday, 1991.

Reid, Ed and Ovid DeMaris, *The Green Felt Jungle*. New York: Trident Press, 1963.

"Reputed Mob Figure Convicted in Scheme to Launder Money." *Las Vegas Review Journal*. Feb 21, 1991.

Rhodes, Robert P. *Organized Crime: Crime Control v. Civil Liberties*. New York: Random House, 1984.

"Riviera Directors Elect Ben Goffstein President." *Las Vegas Review Journal*. Dec. 9, 1958.

"Riviera Resort – Part of Traffic Problem." *Las Vegas Review Journal*. July 30, 1954.

Roemer, William F., Jr. *The Enforcer*. New York: Ballantine Publishing Group, 1995.

Roemer, William F., Jr. *War of the Godfathers*. New York: Donald I. Fine, Inc., 1990.

Schwartz, David G. *Suburban Xanadu. On the Boulevard – The Best of John L. Smith*. New York: Routledge, 2003.

Sheehan, Jack, ed. *The Players: The Men Who Made Las Vegas*. Reno: University of Nevada Press, 1995.

Smith, John L. *Of Rats and Men*. Las Vegas: Huntington Press, 1999.

Smith, John L. *On the Boulevard - The Best of John L. Smith*. Las Vegas: Huntington Press, 1999.

Sonnett, Robert. *Sonnett's Guide to Las Vegas*. Las Vegas: Sonnett, 1969.

Taylor, Richard B. *Hacienda – Hotel History – Supplement.* Las Vegas: Beehive Press, 1990.

Taylor, Richard B. *Moulin Rouge – Hotel History.* Las Vegas: Beehive Press, 1995.

Third Interim Report of the Special Committee to Investigate Organized Crime in Interstate Commerce (Kefauver Committee). New York: Arco Publishing Co. 1951.

Turner, Wallace. *Gambler's Money.* Cambridge: Riverside Press, 1965.

"Twin Slaying Baffles Phoenix Authorities." *Las Vegas Review Journal.* Dec. 4, 1958.

Ward, Kenric. *Saints in Babylon: Mormons and Las Vegas.* Las Vegas: 1st Books Library, 2002.

Wiley, Peter, and Robert Gottlieb. *Empires in the Sun: The Rise of the American West.* New York: G.P. Putnam's Sons, 1982.

Wilkerson, W.R. III. *The Man Who Invented Las Vegas.* Beverly Hills: Ciro's Books, 2000.

Photo Credits

Conquest Collection, pp. 92, 94

FBI Files, Freedom of Information Act, p. 187

Howard Klein Collection, pp. 54, 61, 62, 75, 115, 160

Kim Krantz Collection, p. 135

Lisa Lewis' Scrapbook, p. 79

Lisa Medford Collection, p. 113

NYPD Photo, NY Public Library, pp.16, 78

Oaks Photo Collection, p. 85

Personal Collection of the Author, pp. 7, 20, 29, 44, 46, 47, 49, 69, 70, 81, 88, 105, 128, 147, 157, 165, 170, 173, 201, 209, 214, 235, 237

Riviera Hotel, Courtesy Las Vegas News Bureau. With permission from the Riviera, p. 140

Ruth Gillis Collection, p. 133

UP/Worldwide Photo, pp. 3, 5, 33

Wendel Collection, p. 43

Photo Credits – Some of the aerial photographs in the book were courtesy of either the Las Vegas News Bureau, or its predecessor, the Desert Sea News Bureau. Other photos used in this book come from private collections.

INDEX

I'm Steve Fischer.

Thanks for getting the book.

If you REALLY enjoy it,
here's a deal for you.

Want to send a book to a friend?

It's only $15. If you have two friends, $27.50, and if you are lucky
enough to have three friends to get signed and personalized
copies, $38 for all three! (plus shipping)

Mail orders only (checks or money orders)
or PayPal (Steve@BerklinePress.com)

Shipping and handling
Regular shipping:
1 book, add $3.00 • 2 books, add $4.00 • 3 books, add $5.00

Priority shipping:
1-2 books, add $5.50 • 2-5 books, add $9.50
For larger quantities please inquire

www.whenthemobranvegas.com
Berkline Press, PO Box 32, Boys Town, NE 68010

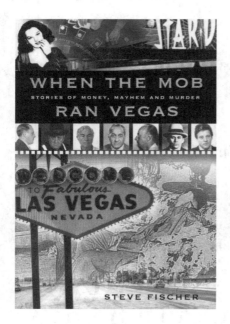

— Coming Soon —
from Berkline Press

Showgirl
Stories

www.WhenTheMobRanVegas.com